Faithful Trailblazers

Missionaries Who Shaped History

Unveiling Inspirational Journeys of Impact and Enduring Faith

By
Alemayehu Mammo

Faithful Trailblazers

Missionaries Who Shaped History

Copyright © 2024 Alemayehu Mammo

All rights reserved

United States of America

ISBN 978-1-61119-114-1

Comments can be directed to the author at
https://www.facebook.com/Alemayehu-Mammo Or
alemayehudmammo@gmail.com or
Call 240-560-2539

Table of Contents

Preface 4
Chapter 1 Philip James Elliot 9
Chapter 2 Amy Beatrice Carmichael 20
Chapter 3 Adoniram Judson 34
Chapter 4 Ann Hasseltine Judson 48
Chapter 5 Eric Henry Liddell 62
Chapter 6 Darlene Deibler Rose 72
Chapter 7 Charlotte "Lottie" Moon 84
Chapter 8 William Carey 95
References 109

Preface

"Are you without a home? I don't have one, either. At 34, I'm living at my mom's place. So, don't use this as an excuse, and don't let frustration take over." This was how I started my talk with six people from different countries seeking a better life but found themselves homeless on the streets of Luton in Bedfordshire County.

Twenty-two years ago, I traveled from Ethiopia to the United Kingdom. At the start, I attended the International Christian Writers and Publishers Conference. After that, I spent an additional two months exploring different cities and talking to people in various churches. Since that experience, I've carried a sense of being a missionary.

While working on an introductory course on missions at the University of the Cumberlands, I decided to put together stories about missionaries. Our professor mentioned that we would be working on various reports about missionaries over the next eight weeks. We had to pick one from a list of eight and share their life stories every week.

I chose to write about these remarkable people and learn from their success during the first week. I focused on individuals like William Carey, Charlotte "Lottie" Moon, Jim Elliot, Amy Carmichael, Adoniram Judson, Ann Hasseltine Judson, Eric Liddell, and Darlene

Deibler Rose. I made sure to follow the guidelines closely.

I briefly introduced the missionaries in each story and highlighted how they significantly impacted mission history. I delved into their early life, examining events or moments that influenced and shaped them. I also explored their conversion experiences and the calling that led them to become missionaries.

Every biography provided an overview of their work before wrapping up with a conclusion. Finally, in each piece, I discussed key takeaways from the person's life. These takeaways helped me gain insights and lessons from their experiences and achievements. A lot has been written about these folks, but the main point is that they've paved the way for us today. I hope you get the same vibes and feel inspired to think about doing missionary work as you read this and other similar books.

The amazing missionaries, whom I call faikthful trailblazers, played a crucial role in shaping history because they followed Jesus's vital task. Jesus told his followers, " Therefore go and make disciples of all nations, baptizing them in the name of the Father and of the Son and of the Holy Spirit, and teaching them to obey everything I have commanded you. And surely I am with you always, to the very end of the age." (Matthew 28:19-20).

These faithful trailblazers didn't just sit back; they took Jesus' words seriously. They traveled to different parts of the world, spreading love and faith. By making disciples, they helped others understand and follow the teachings of Jesus. Baptizing people in the name of the Father, Son, and Holy Spirit symbolized a commitment to the Christian faith.

Not only did these missionaries share the message, but they also took the time to teach others about Jesus' teachings. They helped communities grow in their understanding of faith and encouraged them to live according to Jesus' commandments. In doing so, these trailblazers left a lasting impact on history by spreading the values of love, compassion, and obedience to God's word.

Christ gave the great commission to his 11 disciples, instructing them to go and spread the teachings of Christianity to all nations. However, this task isn't just for those 11 people; it's for everyone who follows Christ, whether as an individual or as part of a church community. In simpler terms, Jesus told his close followers to share the good news with everyone worldwide. But it's not a task reserved only for a select few; it's a job for all of us who believe in and follow Christ.

The job is to tell others about Christ and help them become followers. We can do this by talking to our neighbors and friends and spreading the message in our local community.

However, there's an even more significant part of the job. Christ told us to go everywhere to share his good news. This is called the "great commission." To do this, we need missionaries. Missions are trips where people from the church go to faraway places to tell people about Christ. So, while outreach is sharing the good news with our neighbors, missions take us from our local area to the world. It's ensuring everyone gets to hear about Christ, no matter where they live. And the church makes this happen by sending missionaries on these essential journeys.

Outreach and missions are like two critical pieces of the Great Commission puzzle. It's also like having two essential tasks on your to-do list – you want to check off both to complete the whole mission. They're a bit different based on where they happen, but neither is more important. We need outreach and missions to finish the Great Commission puzzle. It's not just picking one and ignoring the other – it's about doing both together.

Whenever there's a task to be done, there's someone assigned to do it - that's the idea behind a mission and a missionary. A missionary is a person sent out to get a job done. Now, as followers of Christ, we're all considered missionaries because Jesus sends us out on a mission. Sure, some folks feel a calling to travel to far-off places, but the mission begins right where we live, in our own neighborhoods. So, we're all missionaries working to spread the good news, just like Jesus taught us.

Are you involved in reaching out to others? Keep doing the good work! Don't just wait to receive; be a giver, too. Support those out there on mission trips, making a positive impact. If you feel a calling to be on the mission field, don't procrastinate; go for it. And if you're already on a mission, know that a great reward awaits you!

It's super important to remember that Jesus told everyone to go out and spread the word about Him, no matter how old. This means even kids can be part of this mission! We're all like little missionaries. So, when you finish reading this book, could you share it with your kids? Tell them it's a good read, and they should check it out too. Regardless of age, we must keep learning how to do this excellent commission thing.

Alemayehu Mammo

Aspen Hill , MD

(Winter 2023)

Chapter 1

Philip James Elliot

Five men lay still in the humid Jungle, arrows like dark teeth marking their skin. Deep in the Amazon rainforest, their missionary journey ended abruptly, leaving behind questions and a legacy. One of them was Philip James Elliot, a young man driven by faith to reach a feared tribe, the Huaorani. This is his story.

Philip James Elliot (October 8, 1927- January 8, 1956) was a Christian American Missionary who began his mission work in the remote tribal regions of Ecuador during the mid-20th century. Inspired by a deep-seated conviction to share the teachings of Christianity with those who had never heard them.

Nestled in the heart of Portland, Oregon, Jim Elliot was born into a family where faith held the central threads. His parents, Fred, a zealous traveling preacher, and Clara, a respected chiropractor, wove Christian values into the very fabric of their children's lives. Regular church visits and Bible readings were pillars of their upbringing, fostering a deep-rooted foundation of obedience, honesty, and piety in young Jim. Alongside his elder brothers, Robert and Herbert, and his younger sister Jane, Jim learned the importance of living a life devoted to Christ, nurtured by both his parents' spiritual guidance and the vibrant Portland community. This close-knit family environment, brimming with faith and love, undoubtedly played a significant role in shaping Jim's remarkable journey ahead.

Jim Elliot was introduced to Christ at an early age, and he could be seen speaking about Jesus to his friends without any fear. When Jim was six years, he talked to his mother, telling her, "Now, Mama, the Lord Jesus can come anytime whenever He wants and take our whole family because I am saved and Jane is too young to know Him yet." (Philip, J. 2004).

Born and raised within the Plymouth Brethren faith, Elliot's life unfolded amidst a community that sought to emulate the principles of early Christianity as depicted in the New Testament. This movement, originating in Dublin during the 19th century, emphasized a return to simplicity and directness in faith, principles that likely left a deep imprint on Elliot's formative years.

While impactful for Elliot, the Plymouth Brethren movement extends far beyond its personal significance. Renowned figures like the celebrated evangelist Billy Graham, the inspiring musician Keith Green, and the literary giant C.S. Lewis all share this common thread in their upbringing. This diverse group speaks volumes about the movement's potential to nurture talent across different fields, leaving an undeniable mark on various spheres of life.

Philip James Elliot, commonly known as Jim Elliot, was profoundly influenced during his upbringing by firsthand accounts of missionaries who shared compelling stories of life, ministry, and challenges in distant lands. Growing up, he attentively listened to these missionaries as they described the intricacies of their experiences, including the diversity of cultures, unique obstacles faced, and fulfilling aspects of serving in remote communities. This exposure provided him with a wealth of knowledge about faraway mission fields and ignited his imagination, fostering a deep sense of adventure and purpose. Jim actively engaged with visiting missionaries, asking questions and dreaming about his future as a missionary. His youthful aspirations were rooted in a sincere desire to share the message of God with those who had not yet been introduced to it. The impact of these missionaries' visits to his family's home during his youth played a crucial role in shaping Jim Elliot's decision to dedicate his life to spreading the word of God to distant and unreached communities.

Jim Elliot's inspiration to become a missionary was also definitely fueled by the work of early missionaries he admired. From a young age, he was captivated by the stories of dedicated individuals who ventured into unknown territories to spread Christianity. Jim Elliot's inspiration came early from the Work of William Carey, Amy Carmichel, and Brained David (Elliot, E. 2010).

Throughout his life, he attended various educational institutions, and in 1941, Elliot enrolled at Benson Polytechnic High School, where his journey took a spiritual turn. Carrying a small Christian Bible, his resonant voice echoed discussions about Jesus Christ, captivating his friends. Engaging in a multitude of extracurricular activities at Benson, including the school newspaper, wrestling team, plays, and public-speaking club, Elliot showcased his diverse talents as an artist and writer. These experiences not only enriched his high school years but also played a pivotal role in shaping his future as a missionary. The school's emphasis on Christian values and service to others left an indelible mark on Elliot, fostering deep connections and friendships that endured beyond his academic years. Studying architectural drawing at Benson, Elliot embarked on a path that would eventually intertwine his artistic and spiritual pursuits.

Jim Elliot, underwent a transformative experience at Wheaton College in Wheaton, Illinois. Enrolling in 1945 with a desire for total commitment to God, Elliot immersed himself in a daily routine of prayer and Bible study. Wheaton College, founded in 1860 by evangelical abolitionists, provided a nurturing environment for Elliot's spiritual growth, emphasizing the integration of Christian faith with academic excellence.

Graduating in 1949 with a degree in linguistics, Elliot was recognized for his intelligence, athleticism, and deep Christian faith during his time at the college.

Engaging in various campus ministries and organizations, such as the InterVarsity Christian Fellowship and the Wheaton College Choir, Elliot's involvement showcased his dedication to spreading the gospel.

It was at Wheaton that he encountered his future wife, Elisabeth Howard, marrying her in 1953, just three years before his tragic death. They had one child in 1955 and named her Valerie.

Inspired by missionaries' examples, Elliot's Wheaton experience fueled his strong desire to share the gospel with those who had never heard it. His legacy was shaped by the formative years spent at Wheaton College, where he not only pursued academic excellence but also actively lived out his faith through service and commitment.

In the summer of 1947, Jim Elliot's deepening desire to serve God led him to Mexico, where he embarked on a transformative missions trip organized by the Park Avenue Presbyterian Church in Portland, Oregon. Accompanied by his friend Pete Fleming, Jim worked with the Quichua people, engaging in missionary activities and sharing the message of Christianity with those who had not yet heard it. This experience marked the early stages of fulfilling his calling as a missionary. During his six-week stay in Mexico, Jim not only immersed himself in missionary work but also began studying Spanish, a crucial step in his journey. In a heartfelt letter to his parents, he expressed that "Mexico has stolen my heart." This pivotal summer in

Mexico played a significant role in shaping Jim Elliot's path, laying the foundation for his later missionary endeavors. The impact resonated deeply, eventually guiding him towards Ecuador, where he became renowned for his dedication to the Huaorani people, solidifying his legacy as a devoted servant of God.

In 1949, following a spiritually enriching summer spent honing his leadership skills and deepening his Christian faith at a youth camp in Oregon, he embarked on a journey of theological education. The fall of that year saw him enrolled at Fuller Theological Seminary in Pasadena, California, driven by a sincere intention to prepare for ministry. In 1950, after graduating from Wheaton, he dedicated six weeks at the Summer Institute of Linguistics in Norman, Oklahoma, delving into the application of linguistics in missionary work and Bible translation. This period was transformative, as he, along with companions Ed McCully and Bill Cathers, engaged in youth meetings in southern Indiana and Illinois. Simultaneously, they broadcasted evangelistic radio messages on "The March of Truth." Amidst these endeavors, he also collaborated with a missionary in the Ecuadorian Jungle, working with the Quichuas. The experiences in Oklahoma remained fresh in his mind, guiding his steps towards Ecuador in 1952, where he felt compelled to answer the calling of God. Throughout this time, and beyond, he maintained an unwavering commitment to his Christian faith, exemplified by his involvement in various activities that reflected his growing desire to serve God. The winter and spring of 1951 marked a hiatus from his seminary studies as he, alongside Ed McCully, engaged in a diverse range of

activities in Chester, Illinois, including running a radio program, preaching in prisons, organizing evangelistic rallies, and teaching Sunday school. This period encapsulates a dynamic journey fueled by a deepening faith, theological education, missionary work, and a fervent commitment to share the message of Christianity.

Elliot's desire to be a missionary continued growing as he visited Ecuador for evangelical work, where he joined Ed McCully, Pete Fleming, Nate, and Youderian Roger (Akin, D. L. 2012). In 1952, Jim Elliot and his close friend Pete Fleming embarked on a missionary journey to Ecuador, with the initial goal of connecting with the Quechua people. Starting in the capital, Quito, they immersed themselves in the language and culture, eventually moving to the Shandia mission station deep in the jungle after gaining proficiency in Spanish. During this time, Jim focused on developing relationships with the Quechua community, learning their customs, and building trust while honing his communication skills to effectively share the Christian message.

Jim and his friends worked together to reach the tribe of Huaoranians in Ecuador, where they broadcasted Auca phrases to the people as they lowered gifts to them using a helicopter. After a positive response from these people, they decided to settle on a nearby beach.

In 1955-1956, the focus shifted to the Huaorani, an isolated and feared tribe known for their fierce resistance to outsiders. Driven by his unwavering faith, Jim felt called to establish contact with the Huaorani. The missionaries began making cautious attempts to interact with the tribe through gifts and friendly gestures, even learning basic phrases in their language. Jim's approach emphasized building genuine relationships and cultural understanding before introducing Christian teachings, demonstrating God's love through practical acts of service. Documenting their efforts through photos and film footage, the missionaries raised awareness about the Huaorani's plight.

In February 1952, with Pete Fleming and while in Shandia, Jim felt a strong calling to work with the Quichua. He settled with his wife Elisabeth in Shandia, continuing their work with the Quichua Indians. Jim's ultimate desire was to reach the Waodoni tribe, an isolated group in the jungles. With the help of a Waodoni woman who had left the tribe, the missionaries learned the language and, in 1956, successfully made contact with the Waodoni on a sandbar in the Curaray River. This marked the beginning of their attempt to share the love of Christ with the previously unreached Waodoni people.

In 1956, Jim Elliot and a team of Christian missionaries, including NSaint, Ed McCully, Roger Youderian, and Peter Fleming, embarked on a mission to establish peaceful contact with the Huaorani, an indigenous group residing in the Amazon rainforest. Using a small airplane, they dropped gifts as a gesture of goodwill and set up a base named "Palm Beach" near the Huaorani settlement, hoping to share the Christian gospel with them. Despite friendly encounters, the situation took a tragic turn on January 8, 1956, when a group of Huaorani warriors attacked the missionaries, resulting in the death of all five men. The exact details remain somewhat unclear, but it is believed that the Huaorani misunderstood the missionaries' peaceful intentions and perceived them as a threat. Jim Elliot, the first to be killed, chose not to use his gun in accordance with their vow of non-violence. This tragic incident sent shockwaves through the missionary community and the world.

In the aftermath of the tragic incident on January 8, 1956, the bodies of Jim Elliot and his companions were found near the Curaray River in the Amazon rainforest. Jim Elliot's mutilated body was discovered downstream, along with the bodies of the other men, except for Ed McCully, whose remains were found even farther downstream. The rescue team hastily interred their remains beside the Curaray River.

Elisabeth Elliot, Jim's wife, had been warned about the Huaorani Indians earlier, the same group that later killed her husband and the other missionaries in the jungles of Ecuador.

In the aftermath of the tragic incident where Huaorani warriors killed Jim Elliot, his widow, Elisabeth Elliot, and other missionaries displayed remarkable resilience. Despite the violence, their commitment to non-violence and enduring efforts paved the way for a bridge between two cultures. Elisabeth, joined by their daughter, continued Jim's work, fostering a lasting relationship with the Huaorani. Their sacrifice ultimately became the foundation for future peaceful contact with the tribe.

Following the missionaries' deaths, another pivotal figure, Rachel Saint, Jim Elliot's sister, took up the mantle. Undeterred by the challenges, she continued reaching out to the Huaorani, gradually building trust. The tribe eventually allowed Rachel and other missionaries to live among them and learn their language. This marked a turning point, leading to the successful translation of the Bible into the Huaorani language and the conversion of many tribe members to Christianity.

Jim Elliot's life and legacy are deeply intertwined with his unyielding commitment to spreading the Christian faith, a dedication that ultimately led to his sacrificial death during the Operation Auca mission. Despite being aware of the perilous environment he was entering, Elliot displayed extraordinary courage, defying conventional expectations. The narrative of his martyrdom became a catalyst for a paradigm shift in missionary approaches toward indigenous peoples. The Aucas, initially responsible for the missionaries' deaths, were eventually reached with the gospel, illustrating the transformative power of forgiveness. Elliot's enduring legacy encompasses various facets:

his inspiration of a generation of missionaries, a profound impact on cultural sensitivity in missionary work, and a powerful testament to the high cost of following Christ. His story, vividly documented by his wife Elisabeth Elliot in "Through Gates of Splendor," stands as a widely read and influential account of Christian missionary work. Elliot's life and death continue to motivate Christians globally, encouraging them to engage in outreach and missions, especially in challenging and unreached areas. The lasting impact of Jim Elliot extends to the field of Christian missions, sparking discussions on cultural sensitivity, the challenges of missionary work, and the imperative of reaching unreached people groups. His unwavering commitment, sacrificial beliefs, and the enduring inspiration drawn from his story emphasize the absolute worthiness of Christ and the profound call for Christians to follow Jesus, reflecting Elliot's passion for evangelism and devotion to family. In both life and death, Jim Elliot's legacy is a compelling reminder that the pursuit of faith can demand great sacrifice, yet it remains a worthwhile and inspiring endeavor.

Chapter 2

Amy Beatrice Carmichael

Destiny spun an extraordinary tale in the charming village of Millisle, nestled in the green landscapes of County Down, Ireland. Amy Carmichael was born beneath the watchful hills and the whispers of the Irish breeze. Little did Millisle know that a shining light was emerging within its borders. This little girl's journey took her across oceans and cultures to a distant land. The stage shifted from Ireland's lush greenery to India's vibrant tapestry. She answered a calling beyond borders, languages, and beliefs as a missionary. Her story unfolded like an engaging novel in the sacred spaces of India, where she shared faith and a deep love for humanity.

Amy Beatrice Carmichael was born on December 16, 1867, in the small village of Millisle in County Down, Ireland. She was the eldest child of the Carmichael family, returned to David and Catherine Carmichael, and their family would eventually expand to seven children. The Carmichaels belonged to both a religious and a middle-class family.

Amy's personality always shone as a child. She was confident and always game for an adventure, prank, or laugh. Amy was almost certainly behind it if there were giggles at home and school. Her four brothers and two sisters felt lucky to have Amy as their older sister.

At 12, she was sent away to the Harrogate Ladies' College. Harrogate Ladies' College is a distinguished independent day and boarding school for girls in Harrogate, North Yorkshire, England. Established in 1893, it boasts a rich history and holds a prestigious status as an institution dedicated to delivering high-quality education for young women. The college is committed to providing a comprehensive and balanced educational experience that includes academics, arts, sports, and various extracurricular activities.

In the next five years, two significant events would change everything. Amy discovered Christianity at fifteen while attending a Wesley Methodist school.

One pivotal moment occurred when she and her friends participated in an event organized by the Children's Special Service Mission to convey the Christian message to young people. The highlight of the event was a moving rendition of the hymn "Jesus Loves Me," based on the Bible verse John 3:16 (N.I.V.): "For God so loved the world that he gave his one and only Son, that whoever believes in him shall not perish but have eternal life." The speaker led the students, including Amy, in singing these profound lyrics: "Jesus loves me! This I know, For the Bible tells me so." – Amy felt an overwhelming connection with her faith.

This was a poignant moment. It spurred her to make a sincere decision to commit her life to Jesus, a choice that reverberated with the distant prayers of her parents. "He drew me [to himself]," she later wrote, and that experience began to change her in many ways. (Sanborn, 2020).

Amy, the lively little girl, has started to understand that Christ is her Savior and Lord. Building a connection with God brings her immense happiness, and she finds strength in this relationship, which becomes increasingly important to her over time.

In the fall of 1883, Amy Carmichael's life took a downturn as she was compelled to leave boarding school due to a severe illness that left her in poor health. Subsequently, financial hardships forced her to return home before completing her education. The family faced additional challenges as her father, David Carmichael, passed away from pneumonia. The financial troubles continued, leading to the Carmichael family's bankruptcy in late 1880. In the aftermath,

Amy and her mother relocated to Manchester, where she engaged in charitable work among the residents of the slum areas. At just 17 years old, Amy became the mother figure for her family following her father's death, displaying resilience and a bright personality that helped them endure the difficult times.

Amy began by establishing a children's Bible club, inviting kids from her neighborhood to gather and learn about the Bible. At seventeen, her commitment deepened as she started The Morning Watch club, emphasizing early morning Bible study and prayer for its members. This initiative showcased Amy's emerging leadership qualities, proactive nature, and genuine passion for teaching and mentoring. Beyond personal growth, her endeavors signaled a heartfelt connection to the welfare of the less privileged and a dedication to positively impacting her community.

She started going out with the Belfast City Mission to visit the slums, where she made a big difference. This shows that Amy wants to help people and fix unfair societal things. It wasn't only about telling kids about her beliefs, but she actively tried to improve the lives of those struggling. This effort shows how brave and caring Amy is. She went into difficult places to help and comfort people dealing with poverty and challenging times.

Amy's profound care for the "shawlies" showcased her genuine concern for the local girls working in the challenging conditions of the Belfast mills. These young girls, known as shawies, toiled for long hours, often 14-16 hours a day, receiving meager pay and enduring poor working conditions. The name "shawlies" stemmed from the shawls they wore due to their inability to afford warm clothing. Amy's outreach to these girls extended beyond mere sympathy; she actively invited them to the church, organizing Bible studies and activities to impart essential skills.

Amy persisted despite initial discomfort among some long-time church members about the presence of these girls in a respectable Belfast church. Amy's enthusiasm impacted the community, notably demonstrated through her commitment to the shawlies.

Her prayers for the shawlies to discover their rightful place were answered through a remarkable journey leading to the collective acquisition of a building. In 1887, Amy, the driving force behind this vision, secured a generous plot of land from a mill owner, and with a £500 donation from Miss Kate Mitchell, the foundation of the Welcome Hall was laid. This humble tin building became a sanctuary where hundreds of girls gathered to worship the Lord, marking the inception of The Welcome Church. Amy's relentless dedication and successful fundraising efforts led to the construction of a spacious hall in 1894, initially named the "Tin Tabernacle," which later evolved into the present-day Welcome Church. Today, nestled in Belfast, Ireland, the Welcome Evangelical Church is a testament to answered prayers, community spirit, and a flourishing congregation that continues to thrive. The church continues to operate on Cambrai Street in Belfast, welcoming people from all walks of life.

Amy Carmichael endured the physical and emotional challenges of living in Manchester's slums, facing poverty, disease, and violence. Despite the hardships, this period played a crucial role in shaping her faith and determination to assist those in need. Unlike typical missionaries, Amy fully immersed herself in the harsh realities of the slums, renting a room in a rat-infested tenement and experiencing firsthand the struggles of people experiencing poverty. She focused on aiding vulnerable women and children, organizing practical skills workshops and Sunday School classes to empower them and provide education. Amy offered emotional support, spiritual guidance, and a beacon of hope amidst despair, tirelessly advocating for improved living conditions and social reforms, condemning exploitation and injustices faced by slum dwellers.

Amy's unwavering dedication to missionary work took root during a transformative church service. She felt a compelling conviction about the urgent need for missionaries in foreign lands, especially in areas untouched by Christianity. The intensity of this calling heightened during the Keswick Convention of 1887, where a session focused on consecration and surrender to God's will became a pivotal moment for her.

In September 1886, Amy responded to an invitation from friends to attend a summer Christian conference known as a Keswick Convention. During this event, she had the privilege of hearing Hudson Taylor, a missionary in China, deliver a compelling speech. The resounding words "Go ye..." (Matthew 28:19) deeply resonated with her, confirming her calling to become a missionary. This profound commitment was meticulously documented in her journal as being "definitely given up for mission service abroad."

Despite the emotional weight of leaving behind her widowed mother and family, Amy could not ignore the profound conviction that it was God's voice guiding her to embark on this mission. In sharing her inner turmoil with her mother, she likened the experience to stabbing someone she loved. However, recognizing the gravity of the situation, Amy's mother, despite the pain, encouraged her daughter to follow her calling and live her own life.

Amy became firmly convinced of her calling to spread the Gospel overseas and assist those in need. The profound spiritual encounter during the Keswick Convention session led her to describe it as a moment of surrender and a commitment to go anywhere for the sake of the Gospel.

Amy's sincere desire to embark on a mission trip was ignited through her engagement with the Keswick movement. At 22, in 1892, she harbored a solid aspiration to join Hudson Taylor's China Inland Mission. Unfortunately, her plans encountered a significant obstacle when the mission expressed concerns about her health, ultimately disallowing her participation. The setback was rooted in the onset of neuralgia, a painful condition impacting damaged nerves, which afflicted her while she was in Manchester.

This unexpected challenge, however, failed to diminish Amy's determination and steadfast commitment to her mission, setting the stage for the remarkable journey that awaited her.

Undeterred by setbacks, Amy Carmichael ventured into missionary work in 1893, sailing to Japan as the first Keswick missionary at 26. Teaming up with the Church Missionary Society (C.M.S.) under Barclay Buxton, she redirected her path from China due to health concerns. Amy's dedication led her to convert the Japanese captain to Christianity during the journey. In Japan, she immersed herself in the language and culture, successfully fostering relationships and making strides in evangelism. Yet, she encountered a recurring issue seen later in India – a perceived gap between missionaries and locals stemming from differences in attire and lifestyle. Amy's determination to embrace local culture caused tensions with fellow missionaries. Sadly, her health declined after her move to Japan, prompting the mission board to advise her to return to England in 1894, merely a year after her arrival. Although her time in Japan was short, lasting around 15 months, it played a crucial role in shaping her future mission. Amy Carmichael's mission in Japan, from 1893 to 1894, wasn't a long-term commitment, but it significantly influenced her calling.

In 1895, Amy Carmichael made a significant decision that would shape her life and establish her as a notable missionary figure. At 27, she became a Church of England Zenana Missionary Society member, reflecting her commitment to spreading Christianity. In November of the same year, she embarked on a transformative journey to southern India, marking the initiation of a new and purposeful chapter in her life.

Amy Carmichael's departure from Britain on October 11, 1895, symbolized her physical relocation and her resolute decision to immerse herself in southern India's unfamiliar and culturally rich landscapes. Demonstrating a profound dedication to her mission, she left her homeland with no intentions of returning, embracing a life of service and spiritual commitment.

Amy is a person who likes to take charge and get things done. When she came to India, she quickly got involved in her work. Even though she was still learning the challenging Tamil language, she joined a group of Indian Christian women led by a preacher, Thomas Walker. Walker was a straightforward person, dedicated to his Christian beliefs. He started teaching Amy the complex Tamil language, and sometimes, he would get upset when she made mistakes, but Amy would also stand up for herself.

Even before Amy became fluent in the language, she traveled with a group of Indian women called the Starry Cluster to different places in the dusty and dry Indian countryside. They went around talking to anyone willing to listen to Christ and spreading the message of Christianity.

Amy did things differently. She learned the language and culture by doing something unusual—dressing like the local people, wearing a Sari. This was a big deal because most missionaries didn't do this then. Amy was determined to be as much like the local people as possible.

She was very passionate about telling people about Jesus. Her goal was to reach many Hindus and

Muslims in southern India. Even though it seemed like a difficult task, she saw it as something to pray about and dedicated herself to spreading the message of Jesus in places that seemed dark and challenging.

In 1901, Amy founded the Dohnavur Fellowship in Tamil Nadu, India, driven by a deep calling to rescue young girls dedicated to Hindu temples. Witnessing the peril faced by these children, who were at risk of being forced into temple prostitution, Amy established the fellowship as a home and sanctuary. Her village itinerations had made her increasingly aware of the widespread practice where Indian children were dedicated to gods and lived in moral and spiritual danger. This realization fueled her mission to rescue and raise these vulnerable children.

As the leader of the Dohnavur Fellowship, known as Amma (Mother) in Dohnavur, Carmichael's work gained widespread recognition through her writing.

Amy's life underwent a transformative shift when a newcomer, a little girl named Preena, entered her world. Preena had been given to the local Indian temple by her mother. Giving children, especially girls, to the temple was an ancient practice in India. A child would be given as a gift to the gods because of a vow or a family's poverty.

Preena had tried to escape her captors but had been caught and brought back. Her hands had been branded with hot irons as punishment. Planning another escape, Preena had heard of a kind woman in the village who might offer her refuge. She finally found an opportunity to flee and ran to Amy's home. Amy had just arrived back from an evangelistic trip and was able to offer Preena the help she needed. Preena's arrival showed Amy the dark reality of child god trafficking. Before, she had only heard rumors, but now it was in front of her in black and white.

Almost three years after Preena, Amy took care of two babies and a teenage girl. By 1904, three and a half years after Preena had shown up unexpectedly, Amy had become "Amma" to seventeen children- six former temple devadasis. Soon after, Amy and the children needed different accommodations, so the mission she was a part of decided that their property in Southern India, Dohnavur, would be perfect.

As a result, Dohnavur Fellowship was established in 1905. The fellowship, registered in 1927, provided a safe and caring environment, offering education, healthcare, and a Christian upbringing for girls rescued from the dangerous practice. Employees volunteered, and while economic support was received, no direct cash solicitation was made. Carmichael's dedication led to the formation of the Dohnavur Companionship, and her impact extended beyond the immediate rescue efforts as the fellowship expanded its activities to include broader community and social welfare initiatives.

Despite facing health challenges, including a severe fall in 1931 and arthritis that kept her an invalid, Carmichael continued to write and identified leaders, both missionary and Indian, to carry on her work. Her legacy endures as the Dohnavur Fellowship, established in response to the plight of temple children, continues its mission. Through Carmichael's vision and tireless efforts, the settlement in Dohnavur became a place of refuge and transformation for countless children rescued from the moral and spiritual dangers they once faced.

Dohnavur became very special to Amy, and she devoted 45 years of her life to it until she passed in 1951. The numbers continued to grow, and more children came as they put their trust in Christ and could no longer return to their Hindu or Muslim families. They also rescued more children from temples.

They bought more land, built more buildings, established a school, and built a hospital. They eventually added a boys' section after realizing that young boys were also enslaved in the temples.

Amy's life had a massive impact that is still being felt today. The Dohnavur Fellowship grew into a village of a thousand people by the time she died, with staff, volunteers, and children all working together. And the impact of her work didn't end there. Many of the children she rescued and brought into the Dohnavur family grew and took on leadership positions within the organization. So, while Amy's life may have ended, the legacy of her work continues. (Benge, 1998)

Amy Carmichael, a remarkable missionary and founder of the Dohnavur Fellowship, faced numerous challenges in her later years. In 1931, a severe accident left her bedridden, with both legs and ankles broken and her hip and back severely injured, compounded by the presence of neuralgia. Despite these physical limitations, Amy continued to lead the Dohnavur Fellowship from her bedroom, displaying incredible resilience and dedication.

Amy Carmichael's life journey came to a peaceful end on January 18, 1951, at the age of eighty-three. Having served faithfully for over fifty-five years in India, with fifty of those dedicated to the Dohnavur Fellowship, she never married or returned to her native Ireland or England. Her death was attributed to cerebral thrombosis, a blood clot in the brain, resulting in paralysis and ultimately leading to her passing.

Remarkably, Amy Carmichael had requested that no traditional headstone be placed over her grave, and her wish was honored. Instead, the children she had rescued erected the birdbath as a fitting tribute to the woman they affectionately called Ammai, meaning revered mother. The simple inscription reads "Amma," a term of endearment meaning "Mother," symbolizing the deep connection and maternal care she provided to those she saved. So Amy's impact on Dohnavur and the lives of countless children was commemorated with a birdbath erected under a tree at the fellowship.

Amy Carmichael was a particular person who used her pen to create something magical on paper and in people's lives. She wrote poems, prayers, and stories that showed her strong faith and dedication to helping others. She loved India, and her actions left a lasting mark on the world. Amy wasn't just someone who talked about her beliefs; she lived them. She worked tirelessly as a missionary, saving children from difficult situations and building a place of hope with her own hands.

After Amy Carmichael started the Welcome Church in 1889, it stands proudly today, showing the kindness she left behind. The people in the church sing hymns and laugh together on Sundays, reflecting Amy's strong spirit. 2016, they added something more to remember her by – the Amy Carmichael Centre.

Amy's story doesn't stop; it continues like a lively song of caring and meaning. It always tells us that a person's life is best measured by the hearts they touch, not just the words they write.

Chapter 3

Adoniram Judson

In a lonely inn room on a rainy night, an unwell man found himself next to someone nearing the end of his life. Questions and doubts swirled in his mind all day. He couldn't shake off the anxiety and thoughts of death even after a rough night. Alone in New York, having recently moved to pursue a career as a playwright, he had no loved ones nearby. But a few months later, he enrolled in a Theological Seminary and soon dedicated his life to the Lord again. This is not fiction but the real-life journey of Adoniram Judson, a short biography we're about to explore.

Adoniram Judson was born on August 9, 1788, in Malden, Massachusetts, a very old and important city in the United States. His parents were Adoniram Judson Sr. and Abigail Brown. Adoniram Judson Sr. was a minister, and the whole family was known for being religious. Adoniram had two sisters, Abigail and Eunice, and a brother named Elnathan. His family had a big impact on his early beliefs and values, especially when it came to religion.

Adoniram Judson Sr. encouraged his kids to get an education, so Adoniram went to Providence College, which is now known as Brown University. He did really well in his studies there. In 1807, he completed his studies at Brown University, obtained his degree, and took on the role of a teacher. It was during this period that he authored two highly regarded books: "Elements of English Grammar" and "Young Ladies' Arithmetic" (Anderson, 1987).

Even though Judson grew up in a religious family, he chose not to follow the popular beliefs of the time. When he was young, he wasn't sure about Christianity. As he became an adult, he kept questioning and doubting it. Eventually, he went home and told his parents that he didn't believe in Christianity. The question is, why did he make this decision?

There are two main reasons for Judson's decision. Firstly, his natural skepticism and intelligence made him resistant to religious doctrines and traditions, including Burmese Buddhism. He thought it lacked logical support and evidence. Secondly, the influence of his friend Jacob Eames, who held deist beliefs, played a role during their time at Brown's College. Eames made Judson question the existence of God and the spiritual world. Judson started to believe that even if they existed, they had no interest in human affairs.

In 1808, he tried teaching at different places. He opened a school in Plymouth but had to close it the same year. He also worked as an assistant teacher in Boston. Although he finished two books, "The Elements of English Grammar" and "The Young Lady's Arithmetic," he didn't find much success in teaching and had a hard time getting noticed as a playwright in Boston. Wanting better opportunities, he decided to try his luck in the lively literary community of New York City.

In the year 1808, Adoniram Judson had a significant experience while traveling. He stayed overnight at an inn and ended up in a room next to a very sick man. All night long, Judson heard the man groaning and crying in despair. When he found out the next morning that the man had died, he was shocked to discover that it was his own friend and mentor, Jacob Eames.

Before this incident, Eames had influenced Judson to move away from the Christian faith and lean towards skepticism. However, witnessing Eames's painful death and hearing his desperate cries for help deeply affected Judson. It made him start questioning his own beliefs and the emptiness of the ideas he used to follow. This event played a crucial role in Judson turning back to Christianity.

The shock of realizing that the man who led him away from the Christian faith, Jacob Eames, had now passed away brought Judson back to the faith he grew up with. After his return home on September 22, 1808, the next three months marked a swift transformation. He enrolled in the Theological

Institution at Andover, Massachusetts, on October 12, and by November, he started to embrace the hope of experiencing the regenerating influences of the Holy Spirit. Finally, on December 2, he solemnly dedicated himself to God.

Judson enrolled in Andover Seminary as a "special student," still in the process of discovering his commitment to Christianity. Amidst a rising religious fervor on campus, he actively engaged in intellectual and spiritual exploration. The seminary's focus on missions and personal conversion left a profound impact on Judson. During his time at Andover, a significant theological transformation took place, leading him to fully embrace Baptist beliefs and convictions.

This shift prompted Judson to part ways with the Congregationalist mission board that had initially sponsored him. Following his conversion to Baptist beliefs, both he and his wife underwent re-baptism, and he sought support from Baptist mission organizations. Motivated by missionary appeals and the conversion experience of a fellow student, Judson felt a strong calling to engage in missionary work. In response, he founded "The Brethren," a group of like-minded students dedicated to foreign missions.

Adoniram Judson fervently committed to spreading the mission message, drawing inspiration from key books and life examples. One was derived from a sermon titled "The Star in the East" by Claudius Buchanan, while the other, "An Account of an

Embassy to the Kingdom of Ava," was authored by a British army officer focusing on Burma. His perusal of William Carey's account in India also ignited a genuine desire to propagate Christianity in regions untouched by Western missionaries.

In his 1809 sermon titled "The Star in the East," Claudius Buchanan employs the metaphor of the star as a potent symbol of guidance and inspiration. Through this metaphor, he passionately exhorts Christians to follow the illuminating light of Jesus and actively share it with those who have yet to receive its transformative message. Buchanan's theological perspective, evident in the sermon, underscores the global pervasiveness of Christianity. Significantly, his views closely align with the theology of William Carey, particularly concerning the pivotal role of Bible translation in Christian missions.

"The Star in the East" stands out as a highly influential sermon, playing a crucial role in raising awareness and garnering support for Christian missions during the early 19th century. This influential piece contributed significantly to the growth of missionary societies and played a pivotal role in expanding Christianity in Africa and Asia. Moreover, the sermon sheds light on Buchanan's observations of spiritual darkness in India and other Eastern regions, highlighting his fervent belief that these areas urgently require the message of Christianity to bring hope and salvation.

"An Account of an Embassy to the Kingdom of Ava"

by Michael Symes is a captivating two-volume travelogue that chronicles the British army officer's diplomatic mission to Burma in 1795. Symes's exploration was fueled by a prior encounter with the book while researching mission work in the East. Enthralled by Symes's vivid narrative, he was inspired to embark on his own missionary endeavors in Burma. Symes's firsthand account takes readers on a journey from Calcutta to Ava, vividly detailing his experiences along the Irrawaddy River, which he aptly describes as "one of the finest rivers in the world." The bustling city of Ava is portrayed as "large and populous," and Symes provides insightful observations on Burmese culture and society. His encounters with King Bodawpaya are documented, offering a unique perspective on early European-Burmese relations. Additionally, Symes delves into the intricacies of Burmese religious ceremonies, particularly the pwe, making his book an invaluable resource for those intrigued by Burma and the history of Southeast Asia.

Adoniram Judson found inspiration in William Carey's stories about spreading Christianity in India. Carey, often called the "father of modern missions," was a British missionary who worked in India in the late 18th century. His dedication to mission work, translating languages, and understanding different cultures left a lasting impact.

Upon reading about Carey's efforts, Adoniram Judson, along with his wife Ann, felt a strong calling to dedicate their lives to spreading Christianity in areas that Western missionaries hadn't reached. The Judsons were moved by Carey's example and his commitment to sharing the Christian message in unexplored regions. In brief, Adoniram Judson wanted to be a missionary because of the books he read and the exciting stories about William Carey's work in India. The powerful impact of these readings inspired him to actively support and spread the message of missions. Along with his own dedication, this influence led him to become a missionary like Carey, bringing Christianity to places that hadn't heard about it before.

Soon, a deep-seated desire to dedicate himself to missions work in Burma took root within him. However, the prospect of undertaking mission work beyond the American continent presented a unique challenge, as no American had ventured into this territory before. Consequently, he sought the necessary support to embark on this groundbreaking mission.

In the early 19th century, Adoniram Judson played a pivotal role in the establishment of "The American Board of Commissioners for Foreign Missions" (ABCFM). In 1810, he, along with other seminarians, formed this pioneering organization, marking the birth of the first organized foreign mission society in the United States. Judson's influence extended beyond the initial formation as he drafted a persuasive petition that led the General Association of

Massachusetts to officially create the ABCFM, with Judson himself assuming the position of its first foreign missionary.

In 1811, Judson, along with fellow missionaries Nott, Newell, and Hall, was appointed by the American Board of Commissioners to embark on a mission to the East. The following year, in 1812, the ABCFM sent Judson and his wife, Ann, to British India as Congregationalist missionaries. However, during their mission, Judson underwent a profound conversion experience that led him to adopt Baptist beliefs.

Adoniram Judson moved from being a Congregationalist to a Baptist because he started seeing things differently, especially when it came to how scripture should be interpreted. One of the main reasons for this shift was his strong belief in the idea of baptizing believers by immersing them in water. Instead of going along with the popular religious ideas of his time, he followed a path that matched his understanding of Christian teachings.

Friction emerged due to Judson's theological shift, as the ABCFM, being staunchly Congregationalist, did not endorse his move towards Baptist theology. This theological disagreement strained the relationship, ultimately leading to Judson's resignation from the board in 1823. Despite this separation, the ABCFM still recognized Judson's commitment to missionary work and dispatched him to explore collaborative efforts with the London Missionary Society, emphasizing the organization's dedication to supporting overseas missions for nearly a century.

In 1812, Adoniram Judson and other missionaries embarked on a journey to Calcutta, India, and later sailed to Rangoon, Burma (Yangon) in July 1813. Along the way, they visited William Carey, known as the Father of Modern Missions, in India. There, they were baptized by immersion, performed by Carey's co-worker, William Ward. Unfortunately, during their voyage to Rangoon, the Judsons experienced the loss of their first child, who was stillborn. Despite challenges, in July 1813, they arrived in Rangoon, marking the beginning of Adoniram Judson's captivating and demanding journey to Burma, now known as Myanmar. When Judson set foot in Burma, it was an unexplored country, characterized by a closed society with a chaotic dictatorship, a prolonged war with Siam, enemy raids, uprisings, and religious intolerance. Advised by Carey not to visit Burma, Judson, along with his 23-year-old wife of only 17 months, faced suspicion and language barriers as they settled in Rangoon. Over the next 38 years, Adoniram dedicated himself to working with the Buddhists in the region.

Hudson's journey into ministry in Burma was no easy feat; it required a blend of unwavering determination, thorough preparation, and a keen willingness to adapt to an entirely new culture. Over his remarkable three-decade ministry, he etched a lasting impact on the religious fabric of the country. One key aspect of

Hudson's success was his cultural adaptation. To gain acceptance, he immersed himself in the local customs and attire, delving into the sacred language of Theravada Buddhism, known as Pali. Building relationships with scholars and officials, he gradually broke down cultural barriers, fostering understanding and connection.

Facing the challenge of a new and unfamiliar culture, Judson delved into learning the Burmese language, understanding the people's customs and traditions. Even before setting foot in Burma, he recognized the pivotal role language would play in his mission. Months of dedicated study allowed him to grasp the nuances of Burmese grammar, vocabulary, and script, establishing a profound connection with the locals and earning their trust.

Judson went beyond language and customs, actively building relationships with Burmese scholars, officials, and ordinary people. Engaging in respectful conversations, offering translation services, and demonstrating genuine interest in their culture, he created a network of relationships crucial for gaining acceptance and laying the groundwork for his ministry. Recognizing the importance of respect for Burmese customs, he adopted local dress, participated in cultural events, and even studied Theravada Buddhism, showcasing a sensitivity that helped him navigate the cultural landscape effectively, avoiding unnecessary clashes and fostering meaningful dialogue. Today, missiologists continue to study and admire Hudson's methods as a beacon of successful cross-cultural ministry.

Adoniram Judson devoted more than thirty years to his ministry in Burma, facing a multitude of challenges. His efforts were met with adversity, including the heartbreaking loss of his wife, children, and property due to persecution and betrayal by the British Royal Company. Despite these trials, Judson relied on his resilient spirit, a gift from God, to persist in his mission. Throughout his early years in Burma, he encountered opposition from both local authorities and skeptical Christian groups who questioned his unconventional methods and Baptist beliefs. Undeterred, he tirelessly translated tracts and sermons into Burmese, striving to spread his message. Tragedy struck with the death of his wife Ann and several children due to illness, adding to the personal hardships he endured. In a severe test of his commitment, during the First Anglo-Burmese War, Judson was falsely accused of espionage, leading to a 17-month imprisonment marked by harsh conditions and torture. Despite the immense personal cost, his faith and determination remained steadfast, showcasing his unwavering dedication to his mission in the face of persecution and suffering.

Judson faced various challenges in his ministry, but he tackled them with patience and persistence. His mission was marked by a deep commitment to spreading Christianity. Dealing with opposition, he sought common ground, highlighted shared values, and focused on spreading Christianity through love and compassion, earning respect and opening doors for his ministry. Beyond translating words, Judson concentrated on building communities of faith, establishing churches, training local leaders, and fostering fellowship among Burmese Christians, providing vital support for the budding Christian faith in Burma. His impact extended beyond religion, as he compiled the first English-Burmese and Burmese-English dictionaries, contributing to cultural exchange and understanding between East and West.

Hudson made lasting and significant contributions to the Burmese community through his devoted ministry. Notable among his accomplishments are a complete Burman Bible, a Burman grammar, a Burman dictionary, and a Pali dictionary. His impactful work reached far and wide, earning him recognition from both English and local leaders throughout India. Over 37 years of missionary service, he built strong bonds with his followers, who held deep affection and respect for him. Today, approximately 4.5 million Christians can be attributed to his efforts. One of his major achievements was the translation of the New Testament in 1834, followed by the completion of the Old Testament in 1837. Hudson's dedication to translating the Bible into Burmese, including the creation of a Burmese script, stands out as a crucial and challenging task that left a lasting legacy.

Adoniram Judson, a devoted missionary, passed away on April 12, 1850, at 61. After serving in Burma for over 37 years, he embarked on a sea voyage aboard the ship Messenger of Peace on April 3, 1850. Struggling with a serious lung disease, his health had declined significantly. Following his doctor's advice, he was carried aboard the Aristide Marie in the hope that a long sea voyage would restore his health. Tragically, on April 12, 1850, he succumbed to his illness aboard the Messenger of Peace in the Bay of Bengal. His body was laid to rest at sea in the waters of the Indian Ocean. Far from his family and the Burmese church, the ship halted that evening, and in a somber ceremony, without any prayers, the captain ordered Judson's coffin to slide through the port into the night, marking the end of his remarkable missionary journey. A memorial on Burial Hill in Plymouth, Massachusetts, stands as a testament to his dedication and service.

Apart from William Carey, there is another compelling contender for the title "Father of the Modern Missionary Movement" – Adoniram Judson. In 1813, two decades after William Carey's departure from England to Burma via India, Judson emerged as the first missionary from any Christian denomination to dedicate himself to the people of Burma, now known as Myanmar.

Throughout his 33 years of dedicated service, he made only one trip back to New England. In 1813, two decades after William Carey's journey to Burma,

Judson became the first missionary of any Christian denomination to the Burmese people. His impact endures, with over 3,700 churches and 4.5 million Christians in Myanmar attributed to the Baptist mission he founded. His translations of the Bible were crucial in making Christianity accessible to the Burmese. Despite facing challenges, imprisonment, and personal tragedy, Judson's unwavering faith and resilience paved the way for future missionaries. His enduring legacy, woven with threads of translation, community building, and cultural understanding, inspires generations beyond religious boundaries. Adoniram Judson's story continues to resonate, offering valuable lessons for those seeking to bridge cultural divides and make a lasting impact on the world.

Chapter 4

Ann Hasseltine Judson

Her story began with the simple act of reading a book. After finishing it, she resolved to change her life, but it didn't stick. Then came John Bunyan's "The Pilgrim's Progress." This new book left a mark on her soul, and she resolved to walk a better path again. Yet, like before, those resolutions slipped through her fingers. In the cold of winter, She attended conferences regularly, shedding tears as she grappled with her inner struggles. The desire to accept Christ tugged at her, but her commitment to religious teachings seemed daunting. Many thought, and she feared, that success might never be within reach.

Three attempts and numerous others ended in disappointment. But, as the excellent book says, all things are possible with God. In time, she found salvation and became the first American woman missionary. In the pages of Ann's life, broken promises and moments of doubt colored her journey. Yet, with faith, she achieved something extraordinary, turning the page to a new and remarkable chapter.

Ann Hasseltine Judson, affectionately known as "Nancy," was born in Bradford, Massachusetts, to Rebecca and John Hesseltine, who served as a Deacon in a Congregationalist church. She was the oldest among her four siblings, enjoying a joyful upbringing in a devoutly Christian family. Ann had a happy and attractive teenage life. Her siblings included sisters Hannah and Mary and a brother named William. She developed a special bond with her sister Mary, who eventually married Samuel Newell, an American missionary. The Hasseltine family was known for their deep purity and dedication to the community. Although Ann's childhood moniker was "Nancy," she later adopted the name "Ann Hasseltine." Her family's strong Christian values laid the foundation for her later missionary work and profound impact on the world.

Ann Hasseltine Judson was mainly focused on friends and socializing in her younger years, with her father even constructing a dance hall connected to their home. Despite attending the Congregational Church like other families in town, for Ann, it was more of a formality, and her primary goal was to enjoy life. At twelve and thirteen, she enrolled in Bradford Academy, where she encountered more temptations. Parties became a source of pleasure, and the religious discussions she heard daily seemed like harmless entertainment. After a few years of grappling with concerns about her soul's salvation, Ann was wholly immersed in worldly pursuits, unaware of what she was missing. Between December 1805 and April 1806, she spent most of her time on clothes and amusements, drifting in the darkness. Friends worried about her choices, fearing she had little time for such frivolities. Fortunately, this period of waywardness was short-lived.

Ann Hasseltine Judson's path to salvation was marked by persistent internal struggles, resisting peer pressure, and sincere attempts at righteous living. One Sunday morning, while reading a book, a particular phrase struck her heart: "She that liveth in pleasure is dead while she liveth," leading her to recognize her sins and the deserved punishment. Her conviction deepened after reading John Bunyan's "Pilgrim's Progress" at fifteen despite making earnest resolutions and repeatedly breaking them. The cycle of resolution and failure continued due to peer pressure, staining her reputation. However, a pivotal moment occurred during the Second Great Awakening in the early 19th century. Attending religious conferences in Bradford, she wept as ministers emphasized the urgency of accepting Christ for salvation. Feeling the difficulty of adhering strictly to the faith, she finally yielded during an encounter with her aunt, a godly lady. Ann shared her heart condition, received encouragement to repent, and publicly professed Jesus Christ as her Savior at the age of sixteen in 1806, finding forgiveness and embarking on her Christian journey.

In her letter, after she visited her Godly aunt, she eloquently expressed the profound beauty she discovered in the path of salvation through Christ. He emerged as the perfect Savior for her needs, and she grasped the concept of God's justness in saving sinners through him. With a committed surrender, she placed her soul in his hands, fostering hope that she had transitioned from spiritual death to life. This newfound connection with God led to daily communion, a deep affection for Christians of all denominations, and a genuine fondness for the sacred Scriptures. This transformative journey humbled her, challenging her initial self-perception as a lost sinner. It stirred profound sorrow and remorse for her past sins, marking a significant shift in her outlook. Ultimately, she embraced Christ's merits as the basis for her acceptance.

At the tender age of 17 in 1806, Ann Hasseltine embarked on her journey into the professional world by becoming a teacher at Bradford Academy in Massachusetts. This step marked the beginning of her career and showcased her unwavering commitment to education. Ann, known for her intelligence, dedication, and strong Christian faith, saw teaching as a means to impact positively. Her goal was to impart knowledge and witness the transformation of those under her guidance. Ann's devotion was unmistakable as she commenced each day with prayer. This practice even surprised some of her young pupils, as they may not have previously encountered such a sincere and dedicated beginning.

After completing her studies at Bradford Academy, Ann, driven by a sense of duty, continued her teaching journey in Salem, Haverhill, and Newbury, reflecting her desire to share the teachings of Jesus Christ with all. Her journal revealed that, even at this young age, her deepest longing was for people from all nations to know and praise God.

A significant turning point in Ann Hasseltine's life occurred after a profound change in her heart and life. In Bradford, the Massachusetts General Association of Congregational Churches held a historic meeting that led to the founding of the American Board of Commissioners for Foreign Missions. Four students, including Adoniram Judson, went to Ann's parents' house for lunch following this particular meeting, where Ann and Adoniram quickly became captivated by each other. Their connection deepened as they discovered shared interests in missions and a strong desire to serve in foreign lands. Adoniram's missionary zeal impressed Ann, while he was equally captivated by her intelligence and faith. Despite the brevity of their meeting, this encounter marked the beginning of their interest in each other and set the stage for their shared commitment to spreading Christianity as missionaries.

A month after their first meeting, Adoniram chose to express his feelings to Ann through a letter that resembled a proposal, seeking permission to court her. Ann took some time before responding, and instead of providing a straightforward answer, she suggested that Adoniram approach her parents first for their consent.

Adoniram wrote a letter to Ann's father, seeking permission to marry her. It goes like this: "I have now to ask whether you can consent to part with your daughter early next spring, to see her no more in this world; whether you can agree to her departure for a heathen land and her subjection to the hardships and sufferings of a missionary life; whether you can consent to her exposure to the dangers of the ocean; to the fatal influence of the southern climate of India; to every want and distress; to degradation, insult, persecution, and perhaps a violent death. Can you consent to all this, for the sake of him who left his heavenly home and died for her and for you; for the sake of perishing immortal souls; for the sake of Zion and the glory of God? Can you consent to all this, in hope of soon meeting your daughter in the world of glory, with a crown of righteousness brightened by the acclamations of praise which shall redound to her Saviour from heathens saved, through her means, from eternal woe and despair?" (James, 1998)

This was quite unusual in the history of missions. Instead of the usual lovey-dovey stuff you find in love letters, Judson's letter is different in three distinct ways.

Firstly, unlike typical love letters that focus on happiness and romance, Judson's letter talks openly about the tough challenges and dangers that Ann might face if she decides to marry him. He talks about leaving family, dealing with harsh living conditions, possible illness, and even the chance of death. This honesty about the difficulties and the emphasis on sacrifice stand out from the usual marriage proposals.

Secondly, instead of pouring out his personal feelings, Judson sees the marriage as a team effort to spread their Christian faith. He talks about the impact they could make together on "perishing, immortal souls," taking the focus away from their love to a shared higher purpose.

Lastly, Judson is testing Ann's commitment to her faith and willingness to be a missionary by laying out the hardships so clearly. This unique approach shows Judson's dedication to the mission and his search for a partner who shares his firm resolve.

Ann carefully considered Adoniram's marriage proposal, grappling with the challenges outlined in his letter. The idea of leaving her comfortable life for an uncertain future was a significant decision that required thoughtful reflection. Despite the unconventional nature of Adoniram's request and the relatively short duration of their acquaintance, Ann and her family ultimately accepted the proposal. This decision was not just about marriage; it was a calling from God to embark on a missionary journey together. Ann's response showcased her strength, faith, and commitment to a shared purpose. The beginning of her new life with Adoniram marked the start of a journey dedicated to serving God and fulfilling their shared calling.

Adoniram and Ann Judson were initially baptized as Congregationalists, following the practice of infant baptism. However, upon reaching India for missionary work, they encountered Baptist missionaries and studied their beliefs. Convinced by their findings that the Bible supported baptism by immersion for those who consciously chose to follow Christ, both Adoniram and Ann grappled with internal struggles before deciding to be baptized as believers through immersion. The pivotal event occurred in 1812 when they were baptized in the Baptist Church in Calcutta, representing a significant shift in their lives and missionary endeavors. The aftermath brought personal pain and doubt as they anticipated disapproval and potential loss of support. Despite the challenges, their shared faith and commitment to their beliefs strengthened them. Joining the Baptist Church resulted in a permanent separation from the Congregational Church, which had been sponsoring their mission work. Consequently, the Congregational Church cut off their support, leading to a separation from colleagues to avoid conflicting messages. The aftermath marked a turning point in the Judsons' missionary journey, as they continued their work in Burma affiliated with Baptist churches and organizations after their separation from the ABCFM.

Upon relocating to Burma, Adoniram and Ann Judson encountered a challenge in promptly initiating their evangelical efforts – the imperative need to master the local language. Despite this initial setback, Ann Judson's contributions to translation and literature proved to be profoundly impactful. The journey toward linguistic proficiency proved to be a crucial prerequisite for effective engagement in missionary work. Mastering the Burmese language, she was pivotal in co-authoring the first Burmese-English dictionary, setting the stage for subsequent translators and missionaries. This linguistic foundation not only facilitated their evangelical efforts but also became a cornerstone for future endeavors in the region.

Fluent in Burmese, she played a crucial role in co-authoring the first Burmese-English dictionary, laying the foundation for future translators and missionaries. In addition to her linguistic accomplishments, she translated religious texts such as the Gospel of Matthew and parts of the Old Testament, making the Bible accessible to the Burmese people for the first time. She collaborated with her husband Adoniram, who translated the New Testament, and she produced the Catechism, summarizing Christian teachings. Furthermore, she translated the books of Daniel and Jonah into Burmese, and in 1819, she became the first Protestant to translate the Holy Scriptures into the Thai language. Ann Judson's impact extended beyond translation; her writings, including letters and memoirs, provided valuable insights into Burma's cultural, social, and religious aspects during that period. Through her extensive works, she inspired and educated many about "The Role of Missionary Wife as a Calling," contributing to the interest and support for missionary work in Burma.

Ann, alongside her husband Adoniram Judson, significantly impacted education in Southeast Asia during the early 19th century. Ann devoted herself to promoting education, particularly for women with limited opportunities. In an era when female education was uncommon, she actively advocated for and established schools in Burma (present-day Myanmar) and Thailand.

This was groundbreaking, challenging societal norms and opening doors for female literacy and empowerment. Ann recognized the transformative power of education in improving lives and actively engaged in teaching Burmese women how to read and write, addressing the rarity of female literacy in society. She also established schools for girls and contributed to the improvement of the status of women in Burmese society. Through her tireless efforts, she not only empowered women to access knowledge and enhance their lives but also played a crucial role in laying the foundation for the national education system.

Ann Judson's life was marked by substantial personal and professional challenges, which she faced with remarkable resilience and dedication. Battling harsh climates and living conditions, she grappled with various illnesses, such as smallpox, spotted fever, and chronic liver problems, impacting her ability to travel and work effectively. The tragic loss of all three children to illness added emotional devastation to the already difficult circumstances of their missionary life. Ann encountered cultural resistance and suspicion as a woman missionary in a foreign land, hindering trust and relationship-building. The volatile political climate in Burma and Thailand during her time posed a constant threat to her safety. Working in remote locations with limited resources intensified the challenges they faced, compounded by the isolation from family and friends. Challenging societal norms, Ann defied traditional roles for women, actively pursuing education and missionary work, which brought difficulties.

Ann and her husband, Adoniram, both encountered imprisonment during their missionary endeavors, enduring challenging conditions and facing uncertainty about their future. The couple faced imprisonment during the Anglo-Burmese War (1824–1826), with Adoniram enduring nearly two years of captivity while Ann coped with separation, uncertainty, and the responsibility of caring for their remaining children (Encyclopedia.com, n.d.). Despite these adversities, Ann actively fulfilled her domestic duties, providing unwavering support to her husband in Bible translations and writing, establishing herself as a valuable asset to the church.

Ann Judson made essential and diverse contributions in Burma beyond her role as a missionary's wife. She was not just a teacher, translator, and spiritual leader; she also led Bible studies and prayer groups, creating a solid faith community among Burmese women. Alongside her husband, she founded schools to educate Burmese children and worked on enhancing healthcare facilities, striving to improve the overall well-being of the local people. Ann focused on women's ministry and was vital in promoting literacy among Burmese women. Together, their efforts aimed to raise the social and educational standards of the community, leaving a lasting impact in Burma.

Ann Judson passed away at the age of thirty-seven in Amherst, Lower Burma, on October 24, 1826, succumbing to complications from smallpox and a tropical illness later identified as cerebral spinal meningitis. Exhausted by persecution and family responsibilities, she died after the British victory and Adoniram's release. Her final moments were marked by uttering words in Burmese, the language of the people she had grown to love. Subsequently, Ann was laid to rest in Kyaikkami, Moulmein, Mon State, Myanmar (Burma). Following her death, more than half a dozen accounts of Mrs. Judson's life were published, many of which paid tribute to her dedicated service to prisoners in Ava in 1824.

Adoniram found himself in solitude, left to grapple with the sad task of conveying distressing news to Ann's mother. In a poignant letter, he detailed the heartbreaking account of his daughter's burial as follows. "The next morning, we made her last bed in the small enclosure that surrounds her mother's lonely grave. Together, they rest in hope under the hope tree, which stands at the head of the graves, and together, I trust, their spirits are rejoicing after a short separation of precisely six months. Moreover, I am left alone in the wide world. My own dear family I have buried; one in Rangoon and two in Amhurst. What remains for me but to hold myself in readiness to follow the dear departed to that blessed world, "Where my best friends, my kindred dwell, Where God my Saviour reigns." (Anderson, 1987)

After the passing of his first wife, Ann Hasseltine Judson, Adoniram Judson faced a period of profound grief but continued his missionary work in Burma until he died in 1850. During his twenty-four years in Burma, he entered two more marriages, both of which were influenced by the inspirational writings of his first wife, Ann. In 1834, he married Sarah Hall Boardman, a fellow missionary widow whose deceased husband, George Dana Boardman, had also been inspired by Ann's writings. Adoniram and Sarah had five children, but tragically, Sarah succumbed to fever in 1845. Following Sarah's death, Adoniram married Emily Chubbuck in 1846. Known as Fanny, Emily, too, had found inspiration in Ann's writings and had initially been hired by Judson to write a biography of Sarah. Their collaboration evolved into a deep connection, and they married in 1846, welcoming a daughter. However, the joy was short-lived, as Emily passed away from childbirth complications in 1850, just four years into their marriage.

Ann Judson embraced God's call, aware that serving would mean making many sacrifices and enduring a physically and mentally challenging journey. Despite the difficulties, her life stands as proof of the hurdles early missionaries faced and the strong character needed to overcome them. She faced many tough times, but her impact on Christian missions and unwavering faith is remembered.

Ann Judson made noteworthy contributions in missionary work, literacy, women's ministry, literature, translation, education, and healthcare. Her efforts were crucial in establishing Christian missions in Burma and promoting cultural understanding between Western missionaries and the Burmese people. Her legacy remains a significant part of the history of American Baptist missions in Southeast Asia.

Ann Judson holds a significant place among Christian missionaries because of her crucial role alongside Adoniram Judson in translating the Bible into Burmese. This played a pivotal part in spreading Christianity in the East. Beyond her work in translations and writings, she also emphasized the unique calling of being a missionary's wife to the church. Her dedication and contributions to mission work will always be remembered.

Chapter 5

Eric Henry Liddell

Picture this: the 1924 Paris Olympics was like the biggest show in town. The 100-meter race was a big deal, and it was all set to go down on a Sunday. But here's the twist – there was this Scottish runner, a devout Christian who took Sundays seriously. Caught between his faith and the race buzz, he decided to skip the 100 meters. That's a real sacrifice right there.

Check this out: he jumps into the 400 meters, an event he could have prepared for. Tough competition? You bet. But our Scottish friend, Eric Henry Liddell, wasn't backing down. He showed up with pure determination and some hidden talent.

The climax? It's a nail-biting final where Liddell shocks everyone by snagging the gold medal. And get this: he even breaks an Olympic record while at it.

Meet Eric Liddell – a Scottish runner, rugby player, and missionary. His Olympic adventure wasn't just about sports; it became this incredible story of sticking to your beliefs no matter what. Winning in an event he wasn't even planning for? That's the stuff of legends. So, beyond the cheers and medals, Liddell's tale reminds you to stand tall for what you believe in, no matter how tough it gets. That's the real victory.

Born on January 16, 1902, in Tianjin, China, Eric Henry Liddell was the second son of Scottish missionary parents, Rev. James Dunlop Liddell and Mary Isabella Liddell (née Mackenzie). His family, dedicated to the London Missionary Society, included an older brother, Robert, a younger sister, Jenny, and a younger brother, Ernest. The Liddell family's commitment to missionary work in China was evident through the service of both parents.

Eric Henry Liddell, affectionately known as "The Flying Scotsman," had a captivating early life profoundly influenced by his family and upbringing. Raised in a devoutly Christian household, the Liddell family's dedication to missionary work significantly shaped Eric's formative years. Spending his initial five years in China, he was fully immersed in the local culture, fostering fluency in Mandarin and a genuine appreciation for the Chinese way of life. Liddell's childhood experiences in China were pivotal, playing a vital role in molding his character and values. These formative years laid the groundwork for his unwavering Christian faith and commitment to a service life, ultimately shaping the remarkable individual he would become.

At six, Eric Henry Liddell and his eight-year-old brother Robert were enrolled at Eltham College, a boarding school in south London catering to the children of missionaries. This separation from his family instilled in him a sense of independence and resilience, and he mainly reunited with them during their furloughs in Edinburgh, forming a solid connection to Scotland. At Eltham, Liddell displayed exceptional athletic prowess, excelling in rugby and running. He earned the prestigious Blackheath Cup as the top athlete of his year and achieved the remarkable feat of playing for the First XI and the First XV by age 15. He later became the captain of both the cricket and rugby union teams. Liddell's headmaster, George Robertson, characterized him as "entirely without vanity."

In 1920, Eric Henry Liddell enrolled with his brother Robert at the University of Edinburgh to pursue studies in Pure Science. While at the university, Liddell excelled academically and made a name for himself as an outstanding sprinter.

Liddell garnered widespread attention as the fastest runner in Scotland, with newspapers highlighting his track achievements and touting him as a potential Olympic champion. Athletics and rugby played significant roles in his university life, where he participated in the 100-yard and 220-yard races and also engaged in rugby matches for the University Club.

He represented Scotland in various athletic competitions and set several records. His remarkable speed earned him a coveted spot on the British Olympic team in Paris for the 1924 Summer Olympics.

At the 1924 Olympics in Paris, a devoted Christian, Eric Henry Liddell, made a significant sacrifice by withdrawing from his most vital event, the 100-meter run, as the final was scheduled for a Sunday, conflicting with his Sabbath observance. Undeterred, he redirected his focus to the 200- and 400-meter runs. In a surprising turn of events, Liddell secured third place in the 200-meter run and astounded spectators by winning the 400-meter. He set an exceptional pace starting from the outside lane, leading to two competitors stumbling to keep up. His record-breaking victory, clocking in at 47.6 seconds, showcased his athletic prowess and his unwavering commitment to his faith. Liddell's stance on not participating in the 100 meters due to Sunday heats garnered global attention, becoming a central theme in the 1981 film "Chariots of Fire," which depicted his Olympic journey and religious convictions. Despite intense pressure to reconsider, Liddell stood by his decision, leaving a lasting legacy in the history of the Olympics. Even as other runners prepared for the 100-meter race, Liddell delivered a weekly sermon at the Scots Church on Rue Bayard, exemplifying his dedication to his faith and athletic pursuits.

Eric Henry Liddell felt a divine calling to return to China after his Olympic success in 1924. In July 1925, he reunited with his family in Beidaihe, China, where he faced more significant challenges than anticipated. Despite the hardships, Liddell was unwavering in his commitment, convinced that God had called him to this mission. His first role upon returning was as a science teacher at the Anglo-Chinese Christian College in Tianjin, operated by the London Missionary Society. Liddell's journey back to China marked a pivotal moment, as he dedicated himself to teaching and inspiring Chinese students from grades 1 to 12. In addition to his educational role, Liddell demonstrated care and compassion for the community in Tianjin, leading his students in constructing a gymnasium and contributing to the renovation of Minyuan Stadium, which became one of China's premier sports venues. His impact extended beyond the classroom, earning him the title of the father of the Minyuan Sports Stadium.

In July 1932, during his first leave from missionary work in China, Eric Henry Liddell was ordained as a minister in Scotland. This significant event occurred within the Congregational Union of Scotland, marking a pivotal moment in his spiritual journey.

1934, Eric embarked on another life-changing chapter by marrying Florence Jean Mackenzie. The wedding ceremony was held in Tientsin (now Tianjin), China, at the London Missionary Society compound. Liddell's commitment to his religious calling and marital vows was evident throughout his life. An interesting note is that Liddell courted his future wife by taking her for lunch at the Kiesling restaurant, a charming detail that adds a touch of romance to his compelling story. Interestingly, the Kiesling restaurant still stands open in Tianjin today, serving as a tangible link to the enduring legacy of this extraordinary man.

The mission board chairman requested Eric to go back to the area where he grew up. This place had been heavily affected by Japanese devastation, and the people there needed someone to bring them comfort and hope. It's important to note that many Chinese residents in that area held strong negative feelings towards Christians, and missionaries were at risk of being shot without hesitation. Despite the dangers, Eric believed he was the most suitable person for the task due to his connection to the region, so he willingly accepted the mission.

On December 7, 1941, a bit before 8:00 in the morning, airplanes from the Imperial Japanese Navy attacked the U.S. Pacific Fleet and airfields at Pearl Harbor in Honolulu, Hawaii. It was a big surprise because 353 airplanes came from six aircraft carriers. Sadly, more than 2,400 Americans were killed, and 1,178 were hurt. Five out of eight U.S. battleships were sunk or badly damaged, and lots of other ships and airplanes were destroyed. This attack made the United States join World War II on the side of the Allied forces. Even though both countries tried to talk and solve things peacefully, they couldn't, and the war continued.

The attack was a good move for Japan at first, and it happened after many months of problems between the two countries. Japan wanted more land in Asia and the Pacific, making things tense between them and the United States.

The British community in Tianjin found itself subject to the influence and control of the Japanese military during a critical period. Eric Liddell, along with his family, faced the imminent threat posed by the advancing Japanese army, prompting their relocation to a rural mission station. The pressing danger in their neighborhood necessitated this strategic move.

Liddell took on the formidable responsibility of managing the influx of local residents seeking medical assistance and sustenance in their new refuge. The mission station served as a crucial hub for the community, providing a sanctuary from the encroaching military conflict and a lifeline for those in need. Liddell's commitment to addressing the immediate needs of the displaced population underscores the challenges and resilience of individuals navigating the complexities of wartime adversity.

In May of that particular year, the escalating threats associated with the war reached a critical juncture, prompting Liddell to make the difficult decision of sending his pregnant wife and their two daughters to seek refuge in Canada. Consequently, Nancy Maureen Liddell came into the world in 1941 on Canadian soil, tragically deprived of the chance ever to meet her father.

During World War II, Eric Henry Liddell, along with others, found himself detained by the Japanese. Initially placed in a civilian internment camp in Weihsien, China, they were later transferred to a more challenging camp in occupied China in 1943. Despite the difficult circumstances, Liddell, leveraging his skills as a teacher and coach, dedicated himself to serving others in the camp. He educated and entertained children and organized sporting events and various activities to uplift morale. In March 1943, Japan's directive for enemy nationals in Tianjin to prepare for internment in Weihsien led to his captivity. Remarkably, Liddell's influence in the Prisoner of War (P.O.W.) camp was evident as he actively participated in friendly conversations, dividing his time between teaching and organizing youth sports, leaving a lasting impact on those imprisoned with him, particularly the children from the Chefoo School of the China Inland Mission separated from their parents.

Numerous camp internees, including one of his fellow detainees, Stephen Metcalfe, bear witness to Liddell's robust moral character. Stephen admitted, "He bestowed upon me two significant gifts. One comprised his well-worn running shoes, yet the most profound was his baton of forgiveness. He instructed me in the art of loving my adversaries, the Japanese, and in offering prayers on their behalf" (Langdon, 1966). Consequently, Liddell emerged as a significant unifying influence among other internees, alleviating tensions through his selflessness and impartiality.

Eric Henry Liddell, the renowned Scottish athlete and missionary, passed away on February 21, 1945, at the age of 43, in a Japanese internment camp in Weixian, China. Despite having the opportunity to leave through a prisoner exchange program, he selflessly relinquished his chance, opting to provide it to a pregnant woman. This act of compassion left a profound void within the camp, and Liddell's demise, attributed to a brain tumor exacerbated by malnutrition and overwork in the harsh camp conditions, occurred five months before liberation. His death marked the loss of a person celebrated for his strength, personality, and character, impacting the camp's inhabitants, who remembered him as the most famous Scottish sports figure. In his final letter to his wife on the day of his death, Liddell mentioned suffering a nervous breakdown due to overwork, revealing the presence of the undiagnosed brain tumor that, along with malnourishment, likely hastened his demise.

Eric Henry Liddell's impactful journey unfolded chronologically, leaving an enduring legacy transcending borders. Excelling in rugby with seven caps for Scotland and holding British sprinting records, he showcased athletic prowess. His commitment to principles and respect for others resonated, making him a hero and inspiring people of all faiths. Despite sports success, his deep Christian faith remained central, leading him to prioritize religious obligations over personal achievements, as depicted in the film "Chariots of Fire." The Hollywood film, directed by David Putnam, portrayed Liddell's athletic feats, becoming the most significant foreign film in U.S. Box Office history by July 1982, earning £49.4 million in the USA. Choosing a life as a missionary, Eric lived an impactful life, leaving an indelible mark in the sands of time. His story reached millions globally through the Academy Award-winning movie 1982, showcasing his famous quote, "God made me fast. And when I run, I feel His pleasure." Beyond sports and missionary work, Liddell's contributions extended to education and humanitarian efforts in China, leaving a lasting impact on many lives. His legacy is of athletic excellence, devotion to faith, and a commitment to serving others. Eric Liddell's life inspires people worldwide, embodying the ideals of living with integrity and conviction.

Chapter 6

Darlene Deibler Rose

At the tender age of ten, Darlene Deibler Rose found herself enveloped in the embrace of a divine calling that would shape the trajectory of her life. It was a day like any other, marked by the fervor of a missionary convention sponsored by her church. Little did she know that within those hallowed walls, an extraordinary encounter awaited her.

Driven by a curiosity about life in far-flung lands, Darlene attended the convention with a thirst for tales from foreign soils. Yet, there was a deeper yearning within her—a desire to understand the profound changes in her own life since she embraced the teachings of Jesus. Fearlessness, joy in adversity, forgiveness, and mercy had become her companions on this spiritual journey.

The pivotal moment arrived when Dr. Brown posed a profound question to the gathering of teenagers. He challenged them to forsake their families, homes, and safety to embark on a perilous journey to foreign lands, spreading the message of Jesus. A fervent wish echoed in Darlene's heart: "Oh, if only I were old enough to step forward and declare my commitment! But I'm just ten years old."

Suddenly, a mysterious touch rested upon her shoulder. Bewildered, she turned to find no one in sight, but an undeniable presence surrounded her—the Spirit of Jesus. In a soft whisper, she uttered, "What is it, Lord?" The response was ethereal, as Jesus asked, "My child, would you go anywhere for Me, no matter what you had to give up?" Without hesitation, Darlene declared, "Lord, I'd go anywhere for You, no matter what I had to give up!"

In that sacred moment, Darlene Deibler Rose received a divine call that transcended the boundaries of age. A missionary in the making, she embraced the purpose that God had ordained for her life. Little did she know that this encounter would set the stage for an extraordinary journey filled with challenges, triumphs, and unwavering faith. The call was clear, and Darlene's destiny was etched in the fabric of God's grand design.

Born on May 10, 1917, Darlene Deibler Rose spent her childhood in Boone, Iowa, in a caring family alongside her sister Helen. Despite facing challenges like an ailing father and a hardworking mother, Darlene's upbringing was filled with love and support from her parents and sister. The family's home in Boone, Iowa, provided a warm and nurturing environment for Darlene's early years.

At the age of nine, Darlene Deibler Rose's profound

relationship with Jesus began when she and her mom attended a service conducted by a preacher they had heard on the radio. From that day forward, her spiritual journey commenced as she embraced faith in Jesus Christ. Despite facing challenges, such as walking four miles through a blizzard to attend church services, a recommendation from that preacher due to the absence of a car, Darlene's commitment to her faith remained unshakable. Growing up in a Christian household, she wholeheartedly immersed herself in the teachings of Christianity, learning worship songs and absorbing inspiring stories. A year later, the same preacher returned to her town and challenged the participants to become missionaries during another service. It was at this moment that Darlene promised Jesus to embark on His mission.

Darlene was an excellent student who went above and beyond in her studies. She didn't just learn bits and pieces of the Bible; she actually memorized entire chapters and kept them close to her heart. This turned out to be really helpful for her in the future when she faced difficult situations. The Bible verses she had memorized provided her with comfort and guidance during challenging times.

In 1936, as Darlene Deibler Rose readied herself for missionary work with the Christian and Missionary Alliance, she attended a Young People's Rally in Boone, Iowa, where she crossed paths with Rev. C. Russell Diebler. Their meeting blossomed into marriage on August 18, 1937, solidifying their joint commitment to serve on the mission field. Amidst Darlene's studies at Nyack Missionary Training Institute and Russell's home assignments, the Deiblers embraced an opportunity to serve in the jungles of New Guinea. Darlene's journey toward mission work began in her late teens when she initiated studies to prepare for this purpose. Aged twenty, she married Russell Deibler, an experienced missionary in the Dutch East Indies (now Indonesia). Inspired by a shared calling, the couple eagerly embarked on their mission to New Guinea.

Before embarking on their journey to New Guinea, the Deiblers diligently prepared for their mission by undergoing comprehensive training, which encompassed language studies, cultural immersion, and practical skills essential for effective missionary work. This meticulous preparation proved vital for navigating the distinct challenges of the region they were about to enter. In 1938, Darlene, at the age of 22, embarked on her expedition to New Guinea alongside her first husband, Reverend Russell Deibler. Their destination was the secluded Baliem Valley, where they achieved the remarkable feat of being the first American couple to reach this remote region.

In 1938, Darlene Deibler embarked on a life-changing journey, setting sail with her husband to Papua New Guinea, an island lying north of Australia that was intensely mountainous and covered in dense rainforest. The couple embraced a missionary life in this challenging terrain, where hundreds of tribal groups inhabited the region, each with their unique language. As late as the 1930s, the indigenous people were immersed in a Stone Age culture marked by tribal feuds and cannibalism. Undeterred by the harsh conditions and cultural complexities, Darlene and her husband dedicated themselves to their missionary work, initiating a chapter of service that would leave a lasting impact on the people of Papua New Guinea.

After celebrating their first anniversary in Batavia, Java, the Deibler couple embarked on their missionary journey, teaching at the Bible School in Sulawesi, part of modern-day Indonesia. Their mission aimed to introduce Christianity and provide humanitarian assistance to the indigenous people of New Guinea. Overcoming challenges such as rough terrain, tropical diseases, and cultural differences, the couple established a mission station in the New Guinea jungle, fostering relationships with the locals and spreading their faith. Notably, they became the first to bring the Gospel to the Kapaukus people in the Wissel Lakes region of Irian Jaya, Indonesia.

Initially, Darlene worked at a mission station while Russell embarked on extensive journeys to establish a mission base in the remote Baliem Valley. During this time, Darlene immersed herself in language study and contributed to the church and school at the Macassar station. She translated weekly Sunday school lessons, supervised teachers, taught Bible lessons in the school chapel, and assisted the wives of local workers with the kindergarten. In 1940, she took a challenging trek over a dozen mountain ridges to join her husband, becoming the first American woman to enter the Baliem Valley. Overcoming cultural differences and language barriers, the couple learned the local language and shared their Christian faith with the Dani people, focusing on education, healthcare, and spiritual guidance. Their work aimed at improving the lives of the Dani people by introducing them to Christianity. Unfortunately, their missionary efforts were interrupted in 1942 due to safety concerns amid rising tensions in World War II between the Japanese and Westerners. The Deiblers' impactful work continued until the outbreak of war.

After working at the Bible School upon their return to the mission headquarters, the Dieblers faced separation and imprisonment when the Japanese invaded the island in 1942. Initially placed under house arrest, the couple, along with other foreigners, were eventually herded into prisoner-of-war camps, where men were separated from women and children. Captured by the Japanese military after the attack on Pearl Harbor, Darlene experienced the devastating loss of her husband, Russell, who died in a men's internment camp. Following this tragic event, she was falsely accused of being a spy and held in solitary confinement in a maximum-security prison. Subsequently, Darlene endured four grueling years at the notorious Japanese prison camp in Kampili, marked by harsh conditions such as disease, starvation, forced labor, inadequate food, poor sanitation, and physical abuse. Facing a false confession and the threat of execution, she miraculously escaped the sword. Life in the POW camps was characterized by dreadful conditions, with meager food supplies, brutal beatings for small infractions, and diseases claiming many lives. Despite these challenges, Darlene's unwavering faith shone through, and she became a beacon of light to her fellow prisoners, ministering to them and earning respect. Her resilience persisted until the war's end, bringing her freedom after enduring horrific experiences during those four years of imprisonment.

After enduring physical and emotional hardships in a Japanese prison during World War II, Darlene Deibler Rose found freedom when Allied forces, particularly American troops, liberated the internment camp where she was held. This liberation marked the end of Japanese occupation, as the Allied forces reclaimed control of the territory, forcing the Japanese guards to abandon the camp. Darlene, along with the other prisoners, returned to the United States to recover from their ordeals, grateful for the newfound freedom after enduring untold suffering.

Darlene Deibler Rose, after enduring harrowing experiences in a Japanese prison, eventually regained her freedom and returned to the United States. Her journey to freedom was fraught with challenges and emotional turmoil, as she faced the daunting task of rebuilding her life after the traumatic events of captivity. Despite a profound sense of loss, Darlene demonstrated remarkable determination and resilience upon her return to the USA. Reuniting with her parents and sister, who played a crucial role in helping her regain her health, Darlene's unyielding faith left a lasting impression on those around her. Unfazed by fear or worry, she was described by friends as having the strongest faith they had ever encountered and harbored no ill feelings towards anyone. As a widow, Darlene returned home with virtually nothing, yet sustained by grace, she overcame her sorrow and became an inspiring testament to faith and resilience.

Despite facing persecution, Darlene Deibler Rose was compelled by her profound Christian faith and a strong sense of calling to return to the people of New Guinea. Despite the challenges and dangers, she believed in the positive impact she could make through her missionary work, determined to continue the work they had started. Undeterred by discouragement from others, she resolved to return as a single missionary to the island that she believed God had called her to serve.

In 1946, Darlene Deibler Rose was introduced to Reverend Gerald "Jerry" Rose by mutual friends. At that time, Jerry was in missionary training, and through their shared passion for the people of Papua New Guinea, they fell in love. On April 4, 1948, they were united in marriage. This serendipitous connection unfolded amidst unique circumstances, as Jerry had been given a documentary film about Russell Deibler's initial missionary expedition to the interior of New Guinea in preparation for his own missionary work. This cinematic introduction to the challenges and beauty of the mission field further strengthened their shared vision. Following Darlene's recovery in the States, their union became a poignant testament to God's redemptive work in her life, as they embarked together on their mission in Papua New Guinea.

In 1949, Darlene Deibler Rose and Jerry returned to the Wissel Lakes in Papua New Guinea, the very place where Darlene had initially embarked on her ministry with her first husband, Russell. The couple faced discouragement and safety concerns, but Darlene remained resolute. The journey marked a significant return to the region, with Jerry already assigned to a mission post in the Wissel Lakes, echoing Darlene's earlier service with Russell.

For nearly four decades, Darlene and Jerry, accompanied by their sons Bruce and Brian, immersed themselves in a transformative ministry in Papua New Guinea. Over these 29 years, the Roses engaged in tireless teaching, preaching, and diverse tasks, including constructing landing strips and aiding in childbirth. They bravely faced challenges, including encounters with headhunters, while steadfastly guiding people toward Christ. Their impactful efforts resulted in the establishment of numerous indigenous churches and the nurturing of spiritual growth in hundreds of individuals. The Roses also addressed practical needs, exemplifying a holistic approach to ministry. Living among jungle tribes, the family not only led a spiritual life but also contributed significantly to the well-being of the people they served, with a unique touch from their two sons who were born and raised among the native people.

In 1978, Darlene Deibler Rose and her second husband, Jerry, chose to embark on a new chapter in the Australian Outback, responding to the changing political landscape following the Dutch withdrawal from the region. Despite the challenges brought about by the Indonesian takeover, the couple was determined not to retire. Instead, they relocated and dedicated the next 15 years to impactful work with the Aboriginal communities. During this time, they played a pivotal role in guiding numerous individuals to faith and played a significant part in the establishment of indigenous churches, leaving a lasting legacy in the region. After their experiences in New Guinea, Darlene and Jerry Rose continued to actively contribute to their church and the local community in the vast expanse of the Australian Outback.

Subsequently, in 1993, faced with failing health, Darlene Deibler Rose and her second husband Jerry returned to the United States, choosing semi-retirement in Creighton, NE. In 2001, due to health concerns, they made the decision to relocate to Chattanooga, where the joint support of Faith Bible Church and Woodland Park Baptist Church became instrumental in their care. Following retirement, Darlene became a sought-after speaker and author, captivating audiences with her inspiring story.

By 2003, in their 80s, Darlene and Jerry settled into a retirement center in Tennessee. Despite a slower pace, they never fully retired, remaining ever-ready to inspire and encourage those around them to deepen their connection with the Lord. Throughout this period, Dr. Bill Henry, Pastor of Faith Bible Church, and his wife Jan, longtime friends, played a crucial role in their care, volunteering to manage correspondence duties on their behalf.

As Darlene approached the end of her life, she maintained a steadfast commitment to the principles that had defined her existence. During these last moments, she actively engaged in sharing the Gospel, extending her efforts to touch the lives of those she encountered. Additionally, she dedicated herself to supporting and uplifting fellow Christians in their individual walks with the Lord, offering words of encouragement and guidance. Amidst her final days, Darlene continued to emphasize the ever-present nature of the Lord and His benevolence in her life, serving as a poignant reminder to those around her. Her unwavering dedication to these pursuits remained a testament to the enduring values that had shaped her entire life's journey.

On February 24, 2004, Darlene Deibler Rose peacefully passed away at the age of 87, entering the presence of the King she deeply loved and faithfully served throughout her life. Known for her unwavering commitment, Darlene often expressed, "I would do it all again for my Savior." Imagining her reunion with her Savior, one can envision her joyously shouting, "I'm home! I'm home!" Her life was a testament to the sentiment, "She hath done what she could," faithfully serving her Savior until the end.

Darlene Deibler Rose's enduring legacy is marked by qualities of faith, courage, and resilience, exemplifying the indomitable human spirit and the transformative strength of unwavering faith amid adversity. Her story reflects an unwavering determination to live out her beliefs, returning to New Guinea to continue the mission work she and her late husband passionately dedicated their lives to. Engaging in remarkable and multifaceted missionary work, she chronicled her experiences in the memoir "Evidence Not Seen: A Woman's Miraculous Faith in the Jungles of World War II," published in 1988, which has left a lasting impact on readers globally. Despite becoming a prisoner of war, losing her husband, and enduring cruelty, Darlene's life and story continue to inspire countless individuals, encouraging perseverance through difficult circumstances and finding hope in faith. Her legacy resonates through the people she inspired and the enduring lessons she shared, and her unwavering trust in the Lord, expressed in her poignant statement, "Lord Jesus, I'd still go anywhere with you," serves as a testament to her lifelong commitment. Darlene Deibler Rose's profound impact as a pioneering missionary for over five decades is felt worldwide, and her legacy remains a catalyst for generations of missionary engagement across the globe.

Chapter 7

Charlotte "Lottie" Moon

In 1915, the Tengchow Church in China honored a remarkable woman named Lottie Moon by inscribing her story on a stone monument. The inscription tells us that Lottie Moon chose not to marry after school. Instead, she devoted her entire being to serving God. Lottie's commitment wasn't about traditional wedding symbols like veils and orange blossoms. Instead, she embraced a different kind of beauty – the calling of Christ embedded in her soul. Her decision to remain unmarried wasn't seen as an absence but as a strong affirmation that a single life could also be a vessel for God's work. Lottie's life showed that dedicating oneself solely to God could be as fulfilling as the blessings of marriage.

Amidst the whispers of societal skepticism, Lottie Moon's steadfast commitment unfolded as a saga of sacrifice and purpose. Venturing into the heart of China alone, she embraced solitude with joy, sowing seeds of obedience that yielded an immense harvest of spiritual abundance. In the annals of missionary history, Charlotte "Lottie" Moon, appointed on July 7, 1873, by the Baptist Foreign Mission Board in Richmond, Virginia, emerges as a singular figure. At 33, she embarked on a path less trodden, facing the skepticism of an era grappling with "the single woman issue." Undeterred, Lottie, never married, proved that her undeniable qualifications to teach and serve the church eclipsed societal norms, leaving an indelible mark on the landscape of faith and dedication.

Born on December 12, 1840, in Albemarle County, Virginia, Charlotte "Lottie" Moon was the fourth of seven children to Anna Maria Barclay and Edward Harris Moon, both devout Baptists. Lottie's family, of English descent, included two boys and five girls. Raised on the affluent Viewmont plantation, spanning 1,500 acres near Scottsville, Virginia, Lottie enjoyed a privileged upbringing with access to education. Tragically, her father, Edward Harris Moon, passed away in a riverboat accident when Lottie was just thirteen years old.

Lottie Moon's family highly valued education, prompting her enrollment in the Baptist-affiliated Virginia Female Seminary School at 14. She then pursued further studies at Hollins University and the Albemarle Female Institute in Charlottesville, Virginia. Notably, she was the first to earn a master's degree from the Albemarle Female Institute.

Lottie's educational journey was exceptional, especially given the societal norms of her time. At the Virginia Female Seminary, later known as Hollins

University, she focused on languages and literature, showcasing her intelligence and passion for learning. She continued her education at the Albemarle Female Institute, engaging in a rigorous "college-level" curriculum encompassing philosophy, mathematics, and natural sciences. Her pursuit of advanced education for women was groundbreaking.

During her formal education, Lottie Moon demonstrated exceptional proficiency in languages, excelling in her studies with a focus on Greek, Latin, Italian, and French. Her linguistic journey continued as she expanded her skills to include Spanish later in life. Notably, in 1861, she achieved a groundbreaking milestone as one of the first women in the South to earn a Master of Arts degree, specializing in languages such as Latin, Greek, French, and Italian. Moon's linguistic prowess further evolved, leading her to master Mandarin Chinese while serving as a missionary.

The Moon family, deeply rooted in faith, education, and service, imparted strong values to their children. Lottie Moon's life was notably influenced by her sisters, especially Edmonia, who embraced a missionary calling. Despite being raised in a Christian household, Lottie initially displayed indifference to her faith, even rebelling against Christianity during her early years and college days. However, a pivotal turning point occurred in December 1858 when she dedicated her life to Christ and was baptized at First Baptist Church in Charlottesville, Virginia. This transformative experience occurred during a revival meeting at the Virginia Female Seminary (now Hollins University). Lottie's conversion was marked by a profound encounter with God's grace, orchestrated through the efforts of Pastor John Broadus in evangelistic meetings and prayer services. After a restless night that led her to a prayerful encounter, Lottie underwent baptism, reflecting a genuine and profound change in her Christian character just before Christmas in 1858.

Lottie Moon, also known as Charlotte, played diverse roles before her missionary endeavors. Initially, she supported her family during the final years of the Civil War by assisting her mother in managing their estate. Later, she briefly taught school in Alabama, Kentucky, and Georgia. Beginning her professional life as a teacher, Moon attended the Virginia Female Seminary, where she eventually joined the faculty. Renowned for her intellect and passion for education, she began a formal teaching career at female academies, starting in Danville, Kentucky, after the war. Beyond teaching, Moon engaged in educational activism, advocating for women's equal educational opportunities and challenging societal norms. Her commitment to education and service was evident in her multifaceted involvement. Notably, in 1871, she collaborated with her friend Anna Safford to establish the Cartersville Female High School in Georgia.

Lottie Moon dedicated herself to the ministry at First Baptist Church, where she compassionately served underprivileged families in Bartow County, Georgia.

Additionally, she provided financial assistance to a girls' school in Northern China, managed by fellow missionary Martha Crawford. Lottie's commitment to local and global communities showcased her profound dedication to helping those in need.

Lottie Moon's journey into ministry was not a sudden event but a gradual unfolding shaped by various influences. Rooted in her Christian upbringing and characterized by her outspoken and spirited nature, Moon's inclination towards missionary work deepened during college revival meetings. Her pivotal moment unfolded during a revival meeting led by John Broadus, igniting an awakening that propelled her onto a missionary path in her teenage years. Responding to a conviction that God had called her to spread the love of Christ, Moon's dedication to ministry was further fueled by her exposure to global needs, particularly those of women and children, through church and mission publications. Additionally, learning about the impactful work of missionaries like Martha Crawford in China fostered a personal connection, reinforcing Moon's belief in her ability to contribute meaningfully to the mission field.

In 1873, Lottie Moon was chosen by the Foreign Mission Board of the Southern Baptist Convention to go on a mission trip. She went with her sister Edmonia, who was already working in Dengzhou, part of the North China Mission Station. Lottie initially focused on language study, learning Mandarin, and immersing herself in Chinese culture. At first, Lottie taught at a boys' school, but her passion for spreading the Christian message grew when she visited villages with other missionaries. During these visits, she strongly desired to share her faith directly, especially with women and girls.

Lottie Moon's journey into evangelism began during outreach trips to villages with fellow missionaries. Her true calling emerged as she passionately shared the gospel with those who had never encountered it. Despite facing challenges due to societal norms that viewed missionary work as the exclusive domain of married men, Lottie was determined to challenge this narrative and empower women to serve as ministers. Lottie, embracing local customs and living among the people, contextualized the Christian message, earning the respect of the Chinese.

At 45, she fully committed to missionary work in inland China, focusing on places like P'ingtu and Hwangshien. Over the following decades, she tirelessly traveled from village to village, sharing her faith and addressing practical needs by opening schools for girls and providing medical care. Lottie Moon's evangelistic efforts went beyond traditional preaching, reflecting her deep commitment to the spiritual and practical well-being of the people she served.

Charlotte "Lottie" Moon embarked on two significant journeys to the United States in 1892 and 1902, playing pivotal roles in advancing her mission in China. Unlike typical breaks taken by missionaries for rest and reconnection with supporters, Moon's trips were strategically aimed at furthering her mission and garnering awareness and backing. Addressing the challenges faced by fatigued missionaries and advocating for traditional support to Southern Baptist missionaries, Moon emphasized backing the Women's Missionary Union, an essential arm of Southern Baptist missionary work.

During her initial visit in 1892, Moon attended the World's Columbian Exposition in Chicago, an international fair commemorating Christopher Columbus's arrival in the Americas. Leveraging this platform, she showcased her mission in China, connecting with a diverse audience and attracting potential donors. This effort likely contributed to increased financial support for her work.

In 1902, during her second trip to the U.S., Moon, having spent decades in China, participated in the National Education Association (NEA) convention in Minneapolis. Addressing educators from across the country, she emphasized the significance of education in China and advocated for support for missionary schools. Moon's interactions with individual educators helped raise awareness about the educational needs of Chinese children, furthering her mission and impact.

Throughout her missionary endeavors, Charlotte "Lottie" Moon confronted many challenges, enduring revolutions, wars, famine, and plague that significantly impacted her work. Living in harsh conditions with limited access to quality healthcare took a toll on her physical and mental well-being, leading to battles with malnutrition, fatigue, and depression. As a single woman in a foreign land, Lottie grappled with isolation and homesickness, compounded by the loss of her sister Edmonia and close missionary colleagues in China. The cultural resistance to Christianity, political instability, and the prevailing influence of Confucianism, Daoism, and Buddhism added complexity to her mission. Moon faced skepticism, hostility, verbal abuse, prejudice, and even threats of violence from the local population. Navigating the delicate balance of sharing her faith while respecting local beliefs, she confronted societal expectations and gender roles that could have constrained her opportunities. Despite these formidable challenges, Lottie Moon remained unwavering in her dedication, making significant contributions to the promotion of women's education in China. Her resilience, resourcefulness, and genuine love for the Chinese people left a profound and lasting impact, paving the way for future missionaries and contributing significantly to the growth of Christianity in China.

Charlotte "Lottie" Moon's writings, comprising letters, articles, and two published books, serve as a valuable repository of information on her life and missionary endeavors in China during the late 19th and early 20th centuries. In her passionate accounts, she vividly described the challenges faced by missionaries and the needs of the Chinese communities she served, leaving a lasting impact on readers interested in missions, Chinese history, and the remarkable life of this dedicated woman. Her letters played a pivotal role in rallying Southern Baptist women to form mission societies and provide financial support. Moon's extensive correspondence, including hundreds of letters to friends, family, and supporters in the United States, offers a firsthand narrative of her experiences, showcasing her deep faith and enthusiasm for spreading the gospel. Additionally, her formal articles in missionary publications, like the Foreign Mission Journal, conveyed her mission-driven passion to a broader audience. Moon's two published books, "Our One Lord" and "Letters from China," offer a comprehensive overview of her life and work. Beyond these, her unpublished materials, such as diaries and personal notes, provide further insights into her thoughts and experiences. Moreover, other writers have contributed to the understanding of Moon's life and ministry through books, including her letters, journals, and other written works, shedding light on her commitment to Christianity and her observations of Chinese culture.

Upon returning from her second leave in 1904, Charlotte "Lottie" Moon was deeply moved by the dire conditions of people on the brink of starvation. Despite impassioned pleas for additional resources, the mission board, burdened by debt, could offer no assistance. Lottie, selflessly sharing her personal finances and food with those in need, jeopardized her well-being.

Fellow missionaries intervened and facilitated her journey back home in 1912, having witnessed her sacrificial acts, even as she weighed a mere 50 pounds.

Unfortunately, she passed away during the trip on December 24, 1912, at the age of 72, in the harbor of Kobe, Japan. Her body was cremated in Yokohama, Japan, and the remains were sent to her family in Crewe, Virginia, for burial in Crewe Cemetery, accompanied by an official report from the American Consular Service.

In her memory, a monument was erected at Dengzhou Baptist Church in China in 1915, with an inscription expressing gratitude for her love and dedication. Another memorial, set up by the Tengchow Church the same year, highlighted Lottie's lifelong commitment to God's service. In 1918, the Foreign Mission Board's headquarters in Richmond, Virginia, unveiled a memorial recognizing Lottie Moon's remarkable contributions to the missionary field. Further tributes include a permanent marker at Viewmont, dedicated by the Albemarle Baptist Association of Woman's Missionary Union of Virginia on June 3, 1956, marking the birthplace of Lottie Moon. The dedication program included a concise sketch of her impactful life.

Despite her diminutive stature, Lottie Moon, a towering figure in Christian history, dedicated nearly 40 years of her life (1873-1912) to missionary work in China's Shandong province. As a Southern Baptist Missionary, she defied cultural norms by establishing schools for girls and opposing foot-binding. Lottie's commitment to her mission was reflected in her simple and sacrificial lifestyle, where she gave away resources and lived on a modest diet to direct more funds toward the mission. Through her mastery of languages and dedication to cultural understanding, she became a trailblazer for women.

Her legacy is commemorated through the annual Lottie Moon Christmas Offering, initiated by the Southern Baptist Convention to support international missions. Lottie Moon's life teaches us about courage and perseverance, illustrating that challenges should not deter one from pursuing missionary work. The offering, named in her honor, transcends a mere title, symbolizing her transformation from a Christian skeptic to a fearless missionary who inspired countless others. Her enduring impact is seen in the unwavering devotion she showed to the people of China, enduring personal hardships for the sake of the mission. Lottie Moon's story inspires missionaries and Christians globally, exemplifying Christian virtues and leaving an indelible mark on the history of Christian missions. Beyond her contributions in China, her legacy lives on in the hearts of those moved by her selfless service and passion for sharing the Christian message.

Chapter 8

William Carey

William Carey, often known as the "father of modern missions," earned this title for essential reasons. Firstly, he was a big supporter of telling people worldwide about Christianity. He didn't just talk about it; he took action and came up with new and effective ways of doing missionary work. Additionally, Carey wasn't only focused on preaching; he believed in a comprehensive approach. He opened schools and translated the Bible into different languages spoken in India. This made a real difference in people's lives. In this short biography, we'll explore how William Carey's dedication and innovative ideas shaped how we think about spreading the message of Christianity today.

Edmund and Elizabeth Carey, both weavers, welcomed their firstborn, William, in the village of Paulerspury, Northamptonshire. Born on August 17, 1761, in Pury End, William was the eldest among their five children. The Careys, dedicated weavers, had a growing family in the charming Northamptonshire village.

William Carey's early years revolved around the Church of England, and when he was merely six years old, his father assumed the roles of parish clerk and schoolmaster in their village (Smith, G. 2011). Under his father's guidance, William received a primary education that, though limited, laid the foundation for his intellectual development.

Growing up in a financially modest family, William Carey faced limited opportunities for formal education. At 14, due to the family's financial constraints, he began an apprenticeship as a shoemaker in a nearby village. Working in this trade not only provided him with some income but also enabled him to purchase books, nurturing his intellectual interests. Despite the demands of his profession, Carey maintained a solid commitment to self-improvement, consistently engaging in avid reading and self-directed learning.

His innate curiosity about the world, particularly in natural sciences like botany, emerged early in his childhood, complemented by a natural flair for languages, as evidenced by his self-taught proficiency in Latin. Despite lacking formal higher education, Carey's self-directed learning transformed him into a polymath, mastering Hebrew, Greek, Sanskrit, and Bengali languages. His linguistic talents expanded to include Latin, Greek, Hebrew, Dutch, French, and Italian. Throughout his life, Carey's intellectual curiosity and dedication to learning remained central, evident in his continuous scientific pursuits, including collecting and studying plants. This upbringing fueled a lifelong passion for knowledge, laying the foundation for his remarkable achievements as a missionary, linguist, and scholar.

William Carey felt a compelling calling from his strong religious beliefs, a genuine commitment to social justice, and a keen aspiration to disseminate knowledge and education. His focus was explicitly on the challenging situation faced by the people he referred to as the "heathen" in India, whom he believed were living in spiritual obscurity. Carey's calling encompassed a multifaceted dedication to addressing these concerns and positively impacting the lives of those he sought to uplift.

In May 1792, a youthful Baptist pastor, William Carey, released a significant article entitled "An Enquiry into the Obligations of Christians to Use Means for the Conversion of the Heathens." This manifesto urged Particular Baptists to participate actively in foreign missions. Carey argued that the Great Commission from Matthew 28:19-20 applied to all Christians, making missionary work a duty that transcends time. Stressing the urgency of global conversion, he advocated for diverse methods, including sending missionaries, translating scriptures, establishing schools, and fostering financial support. Carey supported his argument with biblical analysis, historical examples, and statistical data, demonstrating missionary efforts' historical precedence and effectiveness in fulfilling the Great Commission.

Although Carey's views on conversion methods have sparked ongoing debates, particularly concerning cultural sensitivity and respect for other religious traditions, his work remains a foundational text for the modern Protestant missionary movement. Despite criticisms, Carey's "Enquiry" continues to shape discussions on Christian responsibility and global engagement, serving as a significant historical text that inspires countless individuals and organizations to participate in international missions.

In the spring of 1792, William Carey received the opportunity to deliver a sermon at the Northamptonshire Association meeting, held by Baptist churches in the region, on May 30. Standing before the congregation at Friar Lane Baptist Chapel in Nottingham, England, Carey drew from Isaiah 54:2–3, urging the listeners to expand their faith and actively engage in missionary endeavors. His sermon focused on cultivating hopeful anticipation in God's power and the necessity of taking proactive steps in spreading the Christian message. Carey emphasized the need to anticipate divine intervention and actively contribute to sharing the Gospel. He stressed the importance of believers extending the kingdom's reach to foreign lands.

Though initially, no concrete action was taken, in October of the same year, a group formed the Particular Baptist Society for Propagating the Gospel among the Heathen, later known as the Baptist Missionary Society. Despite financial challenges,

Carey and his colleagues, including his close friend Andrew Fuller, embarked on missionary work, marking a significant moment in Baptist missions. Carey's sermon not only inspired the formation of the missionary society but also motivated countless others to undertake missionary endeavors, encapsulating the essence of his message with the phrase, "Expect great things from God; attempt great things for God."

William Carey's choice to embark on a mission to India was a profound one, marked by strong religious beliefs, extensive preparation, and triumph over formidable obstacles. His decision wasn't taken lightly, reflecting a deep commitment to spreading his faith in a distant land.

As William Carey prepared to embark on his journey to India, he expressed to his father his readiness for what he considered a profoundly significant and challenging undertaking. In a letter from Leicester, England, to his father, as he readies himself for his initial departure for India, William Carey wrote: "I hope, dear father, you may be enabled to surrender me up to the Lord for the most arduous, honorable, and important work that ever any of the sons of men were called to engage in. I have many sacrifices to make. I must part with a beloved family, and a number of most affectionate friends. Never did I see such sorrow manifested as reigned through our place of worship last Lord's day. But I have set my hand to the plough."

Despite the inevitable sacrifices, including leaving behind his cherished family and dear friends, Carey saw his mission as a noble and crucial endeavor ordained by the Lord. In collaboration with Andrew Fuller, he founded the Particular Baptist Society for the Propagation of the Gospel Amongst the Heathen, later known as the BMS, demonstrating unwavering determination despite opposition. With financial backing secured, Carey, accompanied by fellow missionary John Thomas and their families, he arranged passage on a Danish ship, sidestepping the restrictions imposed by the British East India Company.

In 1793, William Carey, accompanied by his pregnant wife Dorothy and their son Felix, set sail for India, a British colony, alongside a small group of fellow missionaries. This voyage began a challenging journey filled with obstacles and hardships. Carey remained resolute in his mission despite facing illness, rough seas, and opposition from skeptical British authorities. The five-month voyage aboard the "Princess Amelia" was difficult, characterized by cramped living conditions, sickness, and storms. Nevertheless, Carey utilized this time to further his studies of Bengali and work on translating hymns, demonstrating his unwavering dedication to his cause amidst adversity.

Carey's arrival in 1793 marked a pivotal moment in the history of Christian missions in India, heralding new beginnings and endeavors in the region. William Carey, an Englishman, undertook this significant journey to India, eventually settling in the Danish settlement of Serampore, now a part of West Bengal.

Upon landing in Calcutta that November, Carey and his companions encountered numerous challenges, including cultural differences, distrust from local authorities, and limited opportunities to disseminate their religious teachings.

It is notable that William Carey clandestinely traveled aboard a Dutch ship, navigating around restrictions imposed by the East India Company. However, upon his arrival in India, he encountered numerous challenges, far from a warm welcome. Carey, his wife, and other missionaries endured significant suffering. Illness, language barriers, clashes of culture, and opposition from colonial authorities and local religious figures tested Carey's resolve. Carey and Dorothy lost their beautiful daughter, born in India. Carey's family suffered severe poverty at this time without Carey being able to do any job for several months. To provide for his family, he assumed the role of managing an indigo plantation in rural Bengal. Despite these adversities, Carey remained resolute, laying the foundation for his missionary work, which would later flourish.

Carey initiated evangelism, education, and social reform efforts, paving the way for the Christian missionary movement in India. Despite initial setbacks, he persisted, joining forces with fellow missionaries William Ward and Joshua Marshman in Serampore, a Danish colony where they faced comparatively less resistance. Carey's steadfast determination to spread the Christian faith and improve the lives of Indians endured despite the myriad challenges he confronted throughout his journey.

In 1800, William Carey founded the Serampore Mission near Calcutta, marking the inception of the first modern Protestant mission in a non-English-speaking world. Working alongside Joshua Marshman and William Ward, Carey chose a Danish colony to establish the mission due to its greater religious freedom.

This collaborative endeavor aimed to spread the Gospel and instigate social reforms, notably combating practices like the ritual burning of widows. The mission served as a center for printing Bibles, tracts, and educational materials in various Indian languages while providing education to children regardless of caste. It became a crucial site for translating religious texts into multiple Indian languages. Over nearly a quarter-century, the mission significantly impacted India's educational and cultural landscape by setting up schools, publishing textbooks, and advocating for social change. Serampore Mission stands as India's first Christian missionary organization, founded on January 10, 1800, by William Carey and his associates, with its roots in establishing the first Protestant Church in Serampore in 1800 through Carey's initiative.

In 1818, William Carey, Joshua Marshman, and William Ward, founders of the Serampore Mission, established Serampore College in India (Ingleby, J. C. 2000), thereby supporting academic endeavors. This institution, the first of its kind in the country, broke barriers by admitting students irrespective of their caste, religion, or nationality. The college played a pivotal role in shaping modern education in India by offering a diverse curriculum encompassing both Western and Eastern subjects such as literature, science, theology, and medicine. Before its inception, the trio had provided education in the region, including for females. Serampore College's founding principles emphasized inclusivity, with no religious affiliation required for faculty members. Recognizing its significance, King Frederick the Sixth of Denmark granted the college its Royal Charter in 1827, allowing it to confer degrees in Arts and Theology. Led by Carey, Marshman, and John Clark Marshman, the college's initial council, Serampore College became a beacon of educational enlightenment, training generations of scholars, teachers, and leaders in India.

William Carey, alongside the Serampore Mission and Serampore College, made a significant mark not only in India but also globally. Their efforts not only promoted Christianity in India but also emphasized the importance of education, social change, and the exchange of ideas. Serampore College, founded by Carey and his colleagues, became a beacon of learning, fostering education and intellectual growth. Their endeavors paved the way for future missionary movements and educational initiatives worldwide, shaping Indian society through their contributions to education, language, literature, and social reform.

William Carey's impact in India went far beyond spreading Christianity and translating languages; his work for social reform served as a model for missionaries. Motivated by his deep Christian faith and belief in the dignity of all humans, Carey tackled various societal issues. He vehemently opposed practices like sati, where widows were expected to self-immolate, calling it "murder" and "horrid." His advocacy contributed to the outlawing of sati in 1829. Carey also fought against the caste system, promoting inter-caste marriages among his followers and believing in the equality of all before God. Additionally, he championed women's rights, advocating for their education and establishing schools for girls, aiming to provide them with equal opportunities. Beyond these efforts, Carey addressed poverty, famine, and disease by establishing hospitals, clinics, orphanages, and homes for widows, impacting Indian society and inspiring social reformers worldwide.

William Carey's language expertise empowered him to connect with local communities and effectively translate religious texts during his missionary work in India. His dedication to Bible translation was a defining aspect of his life, profoundly influencing the communities he served. With Ward responsible solely for printing and distributing these resources, Carey translated the Bible and other works into Bengali and various dialects, laying the foundation for Christianity's growth in India. His most notable accomplishment was completing the Bengali Bible in

1801, a cornerstone for subsequent translations and the spread of Christianity in the region. Additionally, Carey translated portions of the Bible into Oriya, Marathi, Hindi, and Assamese and collaborated on a Sanskrit translation. He also worked with the College of Fort William to translate Indian classics, such as the Ramayana, into English and authored grammars and dictionaries in several languages. Through his translation efforts, Carey not only made the Bible accessible to diverse linguistic communities but also facilitated cultural exchange and education, bridging Western thought with Indian traditions and fostering religious dialogue.

By 1800, Carey and his team celebrated a significant milestone with their first convert, Krishna Pal, who later emerged as a dedicated evangelist. Despite encountering early struggles, their perseverance gained momentum, culminating in 1,407 baptisms by 1821. While this figure may appear modest considering the vast Indian population, it's crucial to comprehend the formidable challenges and cultural disparities that William Carey confronted throughout his 41-year missionary expedition in India. Carey's missionary work extended beyond preaching; he and his colleagues provided medical care to the sick, fostering trust within local communities. Moreover, Carey laid the foundation for indigenous churches by training local converts as pastors, nurturing Christianity's growth in the region. His impact in India transcended mere conversions, encompassing education, translation, social reform, and cultural exchange.

Carey's dedication, linguistic prowess, cultural empathy, and comprehensive approach to mission work, addressing education, healthcare, and spiritual growth, were pivotal to his success. Carey's legacy reshaped India, bridging Western and Indian perspectives and leaving an enduring mark on both cultures.

William Carey passed away at the age of 72 due to age-related ailments. In his final moments, he directed attention away from himself and towards his beloved Savior, expressing, "When I am gone, say nothing about Dr. Carey; speak about Dr. Carey's Savior." Following his wishes, according to his will, he was laid to rest in the Serampore Cemetery, which was then part of the Danish colony of Frederiksnagore. This cemetery holds historical significance, housing the graves of numerous missionaries and notable figures associated with the Serampore Mission, including Carey himself. His burial site is marked by a modest tombstone bearing the inscription: "William Carey, Born August 17, 1761, Died June 9, 1834; A wretched, poor and helpless worm, on thy kind arms I fall." Despite his significant contributions, Carey passed away in poverty, with his books being sold to support his family. Remarkably, Carey had spent 41 years in India without taking leave by the time of his passing.

William Carey's impact stretches far beyond his achievements, inspiring countless missionaries, educators, and social reformers in India and globally. His life story epitomizes the strength of faith, resilience, and unwavering commitment amidst challenges. Rising from modest beginnings, Carey's journey as a pioneering missionary and scholar left an indelible mark on Christian missions. His endeavors in India advanced religious objectives and contributed significantly to linguistics, anthropology, and natural sciences. Beyond missionary work, Carey's influence was pivotal in shaping the evangelical movement of the 19th century. Dubbed the "Father of Modern Missions," Carey's strategic thinking and enduring legacy continue to resonate in the annals of Christian history. His life underscores the importance of steadfast devotion to God's mission, education, and cross-cultural understanding in contemporary missionary endeavors. Despite his exceptional linguistic and intellectual gifts, Carey's legacy underscores that commitment and empathy are indispensable for impactful missionary work today. Revered as one of the most influential figures in Christian missions, Carey and his holistic approach to missions serve as guiding lights for aspiring missionaries. Numerous institutions and landmarks worldwide, including schools and churches, testify to Carey's enduring legacy, ensuring his contributions remain celebrated and remembered across generations.

William Carey, a significant historical figure, has left a lasting impact beyond his time. His influence is evident in the eleven schools named after him, spread across diverse locations, including Australia, the USA, Canada, New Zealand, Sri Lanka, Bangladesh, and India. In his hometown of Paulerspury, Northamptonshire, St. James Church commemorates

Carey with a dedicated display. At the same time, artifacts associated with him are showcased at Carey Baptist Church in Moulton alongside the cottage where he once resided. Moreover, the Angus Library and Archive in Oxford houses an extensive collection of Carey's letters, along with notable items like his Bible and the sign from his cordwainer shop, preserving his legacy for future generations to learn from and admire.

References

Chapter 1
Philip James Elliot

Akin, D. L. (2012). *Ten Who Changed the World*, B&H Publishing Group.

Bank, A. (2020). Losing faith in the civilizing mission: the premature decline of humanitarian liberalism at the Cape, 1840–60. In *Empire and others: British encounters with indigenous peoples, 1600–1850* (pp. 364-383). Routledge.

Elliot, E. (2010). *Through Gates of Splendor: the event that shocked the world changed people and inspired a nation*. Hendrickson Publishers.

Philip, J. (2004). *The Preacher's Commentary-Vol. 04: Numbers*. Thomas Nelson.

Chapter 2
Amy Beatrice Carmichael

Frank Houghton, *Amy Carmichael of Dohnavur* (Ft. Washington, PA: C.L.C., 1998).

Elisabeth Elliot, *A Chance to Die: The Life and Legacy of Amy Carmichael* (Grand Rapids, MI: Baker, 2005).

Janet and Geoff Benge, *Amy Carmichael: Rescuer of Precious Gems* (Seattle, WA: YWAM, 1998).

Chapter 3
Adoniram Judson

Anderson, Courtney, *To The Golden Shore: The Life of Adoniram Judson*. Valley Forge: Judson Press, 1987.

Bailey, Faith C. *Adoniram Judson: Missionary To Burma 1813-1850*. Chicago: Moody Press, 1955.

Richardson, Don. *Eternity In Their Hearts*, Rev. Ventura, California: Regal Books, 1985.

Chapter 4
Ann Hasseltine Judson

School of Theology. "*Judson, Ann Hasseltine (1789-1826)*" last modified (n.d.), accessed on August 28, 2022

https://www.bu.edu/missiology/missionary-biography/i-k/judson-ann-hasseltine-1789-1826/

James, Sharon. "*The Life and Significance of Ann Hasseltine Judson (1789-1826)*"

James, S. (1998). *My heart is in his hands: Ann Judson of burma: A life with selections of her memoir and letters*. Darlington Evangelical Press.

Encyclopedia.com. "*Judson, Ann Hasseltine (1789–1826)*" last modified (n.d.), accessed on August 28, 2022, https://www.encyclopedia.com/women/en

cyc lopedias-almanacs-transcripts-and-maps/judson- ann-hasseltine-1789-1826

Anderson, C. (1987a). *To the Golden Shore: The Life of Adoniram Judson*. Judson Press.

Chapter 5
Eric Henry Liddell

Langdon Gilkey, *Shantung Compound: The Story of Men and Women Under Pressure* (New York: Harper and Row, 1966), p.192

Eric Liddell: Something Greater Than Gold by Janet & Geoff Benge (YWAM Publishing 1998)

Eric Liddell by Ellen Caughey (Heroes of the Faith series 2000)

Chapter 6
Darlene Deibler Rose

Rose, Darlene Diebler *"Evidence not seen: a woman's miraculous faith in a Japanese prison during WWII,"* Harper & Row, 1988.

Chapter 7
Charlotte "Lottie" Moon

Forten, G *American Authors, 1745-1945: Bio-bibliographical Critical Sourcebook*, 199.

Walton, S. (2010). Charlotte Yonge: Marketing the Missionary Story. *Women's Writing*, *17*(2), 236–

254. (2022). Retrieved August 30, 2022, from http://www.scripturaltruths.org/Articles/Real%20Li fe%20Experiences/

Chapter 8
William Carey

Smith, G. (2011). *The life of William Carey, D.D.: Shoemaker and missionary.* Cambridge University Press.

Carey, Eustance. Memoir of William Carey. 2d ed. London: Hartford, Canfield and Robins, 1837.

Carey, W. (1963). Father of Modern Missions. *Chicago: Moody.*

Bultmann, W. A. (1996). William Carey-(1761- 1834).

Ingleby, J. C. (2000). *Missionaries, Education and India: Issues in Protestant missionary education in the long nineteenth century.* ISPCK.

Dear reader,

I would deeply appreciate a review if you enjoyed this short book because it will help get the book out to many more people. Thank you

www.ingramcontent.com/pod-product-compliance
Lightning Source LLC
Chambersburg PA
CBHW061809070526
44586CB00024B/2779